The Old ALMANAC for Kids

VOLUME 3

YANKEE PUBLISHING
INCORPORATED

The Old Farmer's Almanac Books

Publisher: Sherin Pierce
Publisher emeritus: John Pierce

Series editor: Janice Stillman
Art director: Margo Letourneau
Copy editor: Jack Burnett
Contributors: Jeff Baker, Jack Burnett,
Alice Cary, Mare-Anne Jarvela,
Stacey Kusterbeck, Martie Majoros,
Sarah Perreault, Staton Rabin, Heidi Stonehill

Production director: Susan Gross
Production manager: David Ziarnowski
Production artists: Lucille Rines, Rachel Kipka, Janet Grant, Sarah Heineke

Companion Web site: Almanac4kids.com
Web site editor: Catherine Boeckmann
Activity Guide writer: Faith Brynie
Web designer: Lou S. Eastman
Internet project coordinator: Brenda Darroch
Online marketing manager: David Weisberg
Programming: Reinvented, Inc.

For additional information about this and other publications from
The Old Farmer's Almanac, visit **Shop.Almanac.com**
or call **1-800-ALMANAC**

Distributed in the book trade in the United States by
Houghton Mifflin and in Canada by H.B. Fenn.

Direct-to-retail and bulk sales are handled by Cindy Schlosser,
800-729-9265, ext. 126, or Stacey Korpi, ext. 160

**Yankee Publishing Inc., P.O. Box 520,
1121 Main Street, Dublin, New Hampshire 03444**

ISBN-13: 978-1-57198-495-1
FIRST PRINTING OF VOLUME 3

Thank you to everyone who had a hand in producing this Almanac and getting it
to market, including printers, distributors, and sales and delivery people.

PRINTED IN THE UNITED STATES OF AMERICA

This is the book.
Here is its Web site:

Almanac4kids.com

If you think that this book is fun, think twice—and double your fun at **Almanac4kids.com.** There is more of everything there; for example:

- ◆ see the Moon phases for the month
- ◆ make up a constellation
- ◆ find "best days" for cutting hair, camping, stopping bad habits, and more
- ◆ listen to animal sounds and songs
- ◆ send e-cards to friends and family
- ◆ check out our Web cams
- ◆ do puzzles
- ◆ read posts by other kids
- ◆ send us your ideas for stories

Be sure to check out the Activity Guide, too. It is packed with crafts, projects, games, and ideas—all based on the stories and articles on these pages. While you're at **Almanac4kids.com**, use "Tell Us" to let us know what you think of the site and how you like this Almanac—and anything else that you think we should know. We want to hear from everybody!

Have fun!

The Editors

P.S. Parents and teachers, including homeschoolers, please "Tell Us" what *you* think, too!

CONTENTS

Where Did This Almanac Come From?   8

CALENDAR

Many Moons   10
Lunar Logic   12
The Origin of Day Names   13
Why the Week Has Seven Days   14
Dining by the Calendar   16
When Mules Rule (and Other
    Noteworthy Holidays)   20

ASTRONOMY

What It Takes to Be a Star   22
Something Is Eating the Moon and Sun!   28
The Powers of Attraction   32
Far Out!   36
Giant Jupiter and Its Many Moons   38

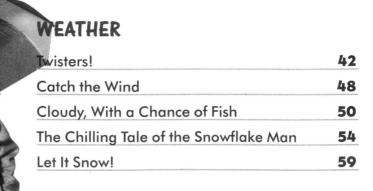

WEATHER

Twisters!   42
Catch the Wind   48
Cloudy, With a Chance of Fish   50
The Chilling Tale of the Snowflake Man   54
Let It Snow!   59

➡ Double your fun: Bookmark
Almanac4kids.com

NATURE

Jaws!	**60**
Beating the Heat	**66**
Food for the Bird Feeder	**69**

THE ENVIRONMENT

Trash Talk	**70**
Ways to Go!	**78**

IN THE GARDEN

Hold Your Nose!	**82**
You Are My Sunshine	**86**
Grow Plants Under Glass	**90**
The Beet Goes On	**92**
Name That Vegetable	**95**
Scrubbable, Lovable Loofah	**96**
Scare Tactics	**100**

ON THE FARM

All About the All-American Bird	**102**
The Buzz on Bees	**108**
Butter Fingers!	**113**

(continued on next page) ➡

CONTENTS (continued)

SPORTS

Got Gear?	116
Baseball's "Cyclone"	120
Hooked on the Outdoors	122
Born to Run	126
Backyard Olympics	130

PETS

Rabbit Roundup	132
Pet-iculars	136
Itching to Know About Fleas?	137
Pets at Work	138

FOOD

Spilling the Beans About Chocolate	142
A Slice of History	146
Honey, Eat Your Ants!	150

HEALTH

Say What?	152
Quick Fixes	157
The Man With the See-Through Stomach	158
Hairs to You!	160

→ Write a poem. Build a model. Have a party, based on a story in this book. These are just a few of the dozens of activities at **Almanac4kids.com/guide**.

AMUSEMENT

Slowpoke's Last-Place Win	**162**
The Kid Who Invented TV	**164**
How to Get Rich Without Doing Any Work	**167**
The Toughest Cowboy Ever	**168**
Bigfoot or Big Fake?	**170**
The Crash at Crush	**174**

USEFUL THINGS

Animal Families	**178**
How Old Is Your Dog?	**182**
What Are You Afraid Of?	**183**
U.S. Presidential Succession	**184**
Metric Math	**185**
Manners Matter	**186**
Birthstones	**187**
Acknowledgments	**188**
Index	**190**

Where Did This Almanac

A true almanac is a "calendar of the heavens." It provides tables that calculate the days, months, and seasons, usually by using the Sun and the Moon. Almanacs of one kind or another have been around for several thousand years.

The earliest almanacs were carved on 12-inch-long, square, notched sticks. Subsequent ones were handwritten on parchment and, later, on paper. The first printed almanac appeared around 1450. "Farmer's almanacs" were helpful not only to their namesakes but also to sea captains and fishermen. As almanacs grew to include many types of miscellaneous information, they became useful to everyday households, too.

These rare, early copies of Robert B. Thomas's almanacs are currently stored in the archives of the American Antiquarian Society in Worcester, Massachusetts.

When British settlers were colonizing the New World in 1675, they brought the idea of almanacs with them. Each local almanac was a little different. In addition to sky and tide information, most contained a calendar, weather advice, postage rates, mileage between places, and town meeting schedules. Some featured curious facts and folklore.

Come From?

One boy who read the early almanacs closely was Robert Bailey Thomas, who lived on a farm in Grafton, Massachusetts. He was especially interested in the almanacs' agricultural advice, but he

also loved to study the night sky and appreciated the astronomical information. He enjoyed a good laugh, as well.

Fortunately for us, none of the local almanacs ever satisfied him.

In 1792, when he was 26, Robert produced a farmer's almanac for the year 1793. He wanted it to be "useful, with a pleasant degree of humor," a combination that no other almanac could claim. He printed 3,000 copies and priced them at nine cents each. To his surprise and delight, they sold out—and he founded what has now become the oldest continuously published periodical in North America, *The Old Farmer's Almanac.*

Robert B. Thomas went on to publish our Almanac for 54 years. We keep his picture on the cover— and show it here—to remind us of how important he was to this Almanac's long history.

We consider Robert to be the grandfather of this *Old Farmer's Almanac for Kids.* We hope that you find it, as Robert printed in his very first Almanac, "new, useful, and entertaining matter."

The very first edition of *The* [Old] *Farmer's Almanac* was published by Robert B. Thomas in 1792. (The word "Old" was added to the title in 1848.) Today, *The Old Farmer's Almanac for Kids* and *The Old Farmer's Almanac* carry on the tradition of usefulness and humor.

MANY MOONS

Years ago, Native Americans kept track of the seasons by observing the Moon. They gave each full Moon a name to describe conditions related to weather or activities of daily life, such as planting, harvesting, hunting, and fishing. Births, deaths, and important events were recorded using the names of the Moon.

SUMMER

Black Elk, a famous Oglala Sioux medicine man, described a special meeting of all of the Lakota tribes that took place during the Moon of the Changing Season (October) and a treaty with the United States that was made during the Moon of Falling Leaves (November).

FALL

Black Elk was born in 1863 under the Moon of Popping Trees. The name indicates the time of year when the pine trees become so cold that they make a cracking or popping sound—December.

WINTER

SPRING

What do these full Moon names, chosen by different Native American tribes, tell you about the seasons, the weather, and nature?

JANUARY
Sun Has Not Strength to Thaw Moon (Algonquin)

FEBRUARY
No Snow in the Trails Moon (Zuni)

MARCH
Moon When Eyes Are Sore From Bright Snow (Lakota Sioux)

APRIL
Broken Snowshoe Moon (Chippewa, Ojibwa)

MAY
Moon When Women Weed Corn (Algonquin)

JUNE
Fish Spoils Easily Moon (Wishram)

JULY
Moon When Limbs of Trees Are Broken by Fruit (Zuni)

AUGUST
End of the Fruit Moon (Cherokee)

SEPTEMBER
Moon When the Deer Paw the Earth (Omaha)

OCTOBER
Moon When the Birds Fly South (Cree)

NOVEMBER
Geese Going Moon (Kiowa)

DECEMBER
Moon When the Wolves Run Together (Cheyenne)

LUNAR LOGIC

Match each month to its Native American full Moon name.

1. January

2. February

3. March

4. April

5. May

6. June

7. July

8. August

9. September

10. October

11. November

12. December

a. Moon When the Horses Get Fat (Cheyenne)

b. Moon When Young Ducks Begin to Fly (Cree)

c. Moon When the Hot Weather Begins (Northern Arapaho)

d. Frost in the Teepee Moon (Sioux)

e. Falling Leaves Moon (Chippewa, Ojibwa)

f. Whispering Wind Moon (Hopi)

g. Moon When the Rivers Begin to Freeze (Cree)

h. Ice Breaking in the River Moon (Northern Arapaho)

i. Big Winter Moon (Creek)

j. Middle of Summer Moon (Ponca)

k. Bone Moon (when there is so little food that people gnaw on bones and eat bone marrow soup) (Eastern Cherokee)

l. Moon When the Calves Grow Hair (Sioux)

Answers: 1. d; 2. k; 3. f; 4. h; 5. a; 6. c; 7. j; 8. b; 9. l; 10. e; 11. g; 12. i

The Origin of DAY NAMES

The days of the week were named by ancient Romans with the Latin words for the Sun, the Moon, and the five known planets. These names have survived in European languages, but English names also reflect Anglo-Saxon and Norse influences.

ENGLISH	LATIN	FRENCH	ITALIAN	SPANISH	ANGLO-SAXON AND NORSE
SUNDAY	dies Solis (Sol's day)	dimanche	domenica	domingo	Sunnandæg (Sun's day)
		from the Latin for "Lord's day"			
MONDAY	dies Lunae (Luna's day)	lundi	lunedì	lunes	Monandæg (Moon's day)
TUESDAY	dies Martis (Mars's day)	mardi	martedì	martes	Tiwesdæg (Tiw's day)
WEDNESDAY	dies Mercurii (Mercury's day)	mercredi	mercoledì	miércoles	Wodnesdæg (Woden's day)
THURSDAY	dies Jovis (Jupiter's day)	jeudi	giovedì	jueves	Thursdæg (Thor's day)
FRIDAY	dies Veneris (Venus's day)	vendredi	venerdì	viernes	Frigedæg (Frigga's day)
SATURDAY	dies Saturni (Saturn's day)	samedi	sabato	sábado	Saeterndæg (Saturn's day)
		from the Latin for "Sabbath"			

Why the WEEK Has SEVEN DAYS

There really is no reason— it's just that nothing else seems to work as well.

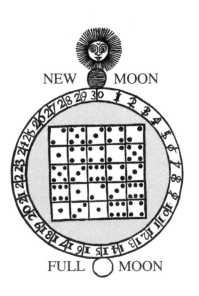

NEW MOON

FULL MOON

The length of a year corresponds to the movement of Earth around the Sun, and the length of a month corresponds to the Moon's revolution around Earth, but what about the length of a week? It makes no astronomical sense whatsoever.

A week is roughly the length of a phase of the Moon—7 days, 9 hours.

But centuries ago, as those 9 hours piled up, they caused chronographic chaos. To create order, people devised solutions.

Astrologers in Mesopotamia, one of the earliest civilizations in the Middle East, created the first 7-day week when they designated one day for each of the seven most prominent objects in the sky: the Sun, the Moon, and the five major planets visible to the naked eye.

Early Jews also adopted a 7-day week but based it on the 6 days that it took the Lord to create the universe, as reported in the Book of Genesis in the Scriptures. We can thank them for adding the first regularly scheduled day of observance unrelated to natural phenomena—the Sabbath, or day of rest.

In some ancient societies, the market schedule determined the length of a week. In West Africa, a week was 4 days; in Assyria, it was 6 days; in Rome, 8; in Egypt, 10; in China, 15.

In 1793, the leaders of the French Revolution produced a calendar with three 10-day periods in each month. It never caught on, so Napoleon abandoned it in 1806.

In 1929, officials in the Soviet Union (which included Russia) invented a 5-day week based on the colors yellow, orange, red, purple, and green. Each citizen was assigned a color as his or her day off. It didn't last. In 1932, numbers replaced colors and the week was extended to 6 days. This also failed, and by 1940 Soviets were using 7 days like the rest of the world.

Mathematically, a 7-day week makes no sense, either. It doesn't divide evenly into a 365- or 366-day year, and many holidays fall on different days of the week each year. But this makes most people happy. After all, would you want your birthday to be on the same day of the week forever?

DINING BY

ON CERTAIN DAYS, we celebrate and commemorate people and events by eating traditional foods. Here are a few not-so-well-known culinary customs:

January

On **EPIPHANY** (January 6), people eat a cake with a lucky bean baked in it. Whoever finds the bean is the king of the feast, in memory of the three kings who traveled to find baby Jesus on this day.

ROBERT BURNS DAY (January 25, his birthday) is celebrated in Scotland and by Scots living elsewhere. Burns wrote "Auld Lang Syne" and other poems. The traditional Scottish dish is haggis—sheep's stomach stuffed with suet, chopped organ meat (heart, lungs, liver), onions, oatmeal, and seasonings.

February or March

Pancakes are traditionally made and eaten on **SHROVE TUESDAY** to use up the last of the eggs and butter before the 40-day fast of Lent begins on the next day, Ash Wednesday.

In early paintings, **ST. AGATHA** appears to be carrying loaves of bread on a platter. In southern Europe, round loaves of bread are blessed by a priest and eaten on her feast day (February 5).

HE CALENDAR

March or April

Eggs represent a new beginning, new life, and **EASTER.** In Italy, people celebrate with *pizza chiena,* an egg-based crust filled with ricotta, mozzarella, and Italian meats.

Hamantaschen, three-corner cookies often flavored with poppy seeds and fruit preserves, are eaten on **PURIM,** which celebrates the day that the Jews were liberated from Haman, a dictator who persecuted them and, it is said, wore a three-corner hat.

May

In southern Europe, dove or pigeon is eaten on the seventh Sunday after Easter, or **WHITSUNDAY (PENTECOST),** in honor of the Holy Spirit.

June

In Sweden, people celebrate the **SUMMER SOLSTICE** (around June 21) by eating the first strawberries of the season.

CONTINUED

July

Centuries ago, St. Swithin miraculously restored a basket of eggs that had been broken by a poor woman who was taking them to market. Eggs are traditionally eaten on **ST. SWITHIN'S DAY** (July 15).

August

LAMMAS DAY (August 1) marks the beginning of the harvest. In old England, loaves of bread were baked from the ripened grain, consecrated in churches, and eaten.

Oysters are eaten on **ST. JAMES'S DAY** (July 25) because he was a fisherman.

September or October

During the Jewish observation of **ROSH HASHANAH,** honey and foods colored orange or yellow are eaten to symbolize a bright, joyous, and sweet new year.

Cold meat is eaten on **ST. LAWRENCE'S DAY** (August 10) because he was roasted to death on a grill.

In medieval England, apples and nuts were believed to have magical powers and so were eaten on **HALLOWEEN** (October 31).

October

November

On **ALL SAINTS' DAY** (November 1), doughnuts called soul cakes are eaten. This stems from an old English custom of going "souling" (singing) door-to-door to beg for cakes in remembrance of the dead.

Beans, peas, and lentils, considered food of the poor, were customarily eaten on **ALL SOULS' DAY** (November 2). Also known as the Day of the Dead, this is a time when children in Spanish-speaking countries eat sugar candies shaped like human skulls.

In Germany, children are given fruit, nuts, and candy on **ST. NICHOLAS'S DAY** (December 6) to commemorate the kindness and gifts that he showered on young people.

December

During **KWANZAA** (which starts on December 26), traditional African cuisine, such as beef and peanut stew and sweet potato fritters, is eaten.

Do you have a special food that you and your family eat to celebrate or remember a special occasion? Share it at Almanac4kids.com/tellus.

When MULES RULE

MULE DAY

IN APRIL in Columbia, Tennessee, mules rule.
During the 1800s, before tractors were invented, mules were valuable assets to farmers and Columbia was famous for its healthy mule stock. The Mule Day tradition began in 1840, when large crowds would come to the town for live-stock shows and mule markets. Today, the festival (usually in the first week in April) includes a mule parade, arts and crafts, mule shows, flea markets, and a church service.

CINCO DE MAYO

MAY 5 (*Cinco de Mayo* in Spanish) celebrates a Mexican military victory. In 1862, the French army was marching to Mexico City to establish a French empire. The weary soldiers never completed the journey. On May 5, while resting at the town of Puebla, they were attacked and defeated by the Mexican army. Today, the Battle of Puebla is commemorated with Mexican food, festivals, parades, and piñatas.

JUNETEENTH

JUNE 19, also called Emancipation Day, recognizes the end of slavery in Texas. On this day in 1865, Union major general Gordon Granger arrived with federal troops in Galveston to enforce the Emancipation Proclamation issued by President Abraham Lincoln on January 1, 1863. Some 250,000 people were freed. Juneteenth (from the words "June" and "nineteenth") is celebrated with picnics, parades, and dances.

(and ☼ther Noteworthy Holidays)

Need a reason to celebrate? Mark your calendar for these . . .

Fun Times

January 24	Belly Laugh Day	Make someone smile, giggle, or laugh out loud.
February 13	Get a Different Name Day	Change your given name, just for today.
March 23	National Puppy Day	Appreciate puppies and raise puppy adoption awareness.
April 12	National Licorice Day	Eat black licorice and celebrate its health benefits.
May 8	No Socks Day	Help the environment by making less laundry to do.
June 19 (2010)*	World Juggling Day	Demonstrate, teach, and enjoy the art of juggling.
July 23	Hot Enough for Ya? Day	Utter this phrase when the July heat sets in.
August 1	Respect for Parents Day	Honor your parents for all that they do for you.
September 10	Swap Ideas Day	Encourage the spread of creative thinking.
October 31	National Knock-Knock Day	Make up three knock-knock jokes and tell them to your friends.
November 29	Electronic Greeting Day	Save paper by contacting someone electronically.
December 31	Make Up Your Mind Day	Make a decision and stick with it.

always celebrated on the Saturday closest to June 17, founding day of the International Jugglers Association

The Almanac makes every day special. See what makes today, this week, and this month special at Almanac4kids.com/calendar.

What It Takes to Be a

STAR

More than 100 billion stars exist in our galaxy, yet on a clear night only about 3,000 of them are visible to the naked eye.

STAR BRIGHT

★ **A** bright star, as seen from Earth, is either closer to us than other stars or produces more energy—or both.

★ **A**stronomers rate star brightness by magnitude. Magnitude 1 is about 100 times brighter than magnitude 6.

★ **S**tars with a magnitude of 6 or less can be seen with the naked eye.

★ **T**he brightest star seen from Earth, Sirius, is magnitude –1.46.

For Good Luck...

Make a wish on the first star you see at night:

Star light, star bright,
First star I see tonight,
I wish I may, I wish I might,
Have the wish I wish tonight.

Light from an explosion illuminates dust around the star
V838 Moncerotis, 20,000 light-years away from Earth.

ALL STARS ARE NOT WHITE

★ The color of a star indicates the temperature at its surface. The hottest stars are blue. The coolest stars are red. (Think of a candle flame. The hottest area is blue!) Astronomers have sorted star colors into classes. More stars are red than any other color.

continued

A Rainbow of Stars

CLASS	COLOR	TEMPERATURE	STAR
O	Blue	30,000–60,000 K	Delta Orionis
B	Bluish white	10,000–30,000 K	Rigel
A	White	7,500–10,000 K	Sirius
F	Yellowish white	6,000–7,500 K	Fomalhaut
G	Yellow	5,000–6,000 K	Sun
K	Orange	3,500–5,000 K	Arcturus
M	Red	2,000–3,500 K	Betelgeuse

Star temperature is measured on the KELVIN SCALE:
0 (zero) K = –459.67° Fahrenheit = –273.15° Celsius

HOW STARS ARE BORN

★ Stars form in dense billows of gas and dust particles called GIANT MOLECULAR CLOUDS. Gravity constantly pulls the particles together, while pressure constantly pushes them apart, until the molecular cloud cools. The particles then gather into clumps called PROTOSTARS. Gathering creates heat, and some protostars become so hot that they release energy (a process called thermonuclear fusion). This gathering and releasing balances a protostar, and it begins evolving into a star like the Sun.

A protostar that is too small to become a star is called a BROWN DWARF. It produces heat for a few million years.

Each fingerlike projection of this giant molecular cloud in the Eagle Nebula is larger than our solar system.

SUPER STARS

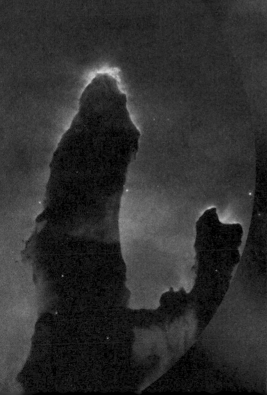

Hypergiant star Canis Majoris

A star can shrink or grow. Small stars last longer than large stars.

Stars usually begin as dwarf stars. These are small, but they can last for millions (even billions) of years. The Sun is a dwarf star.

DWARF stars can become giants, supergiants, or hypergiants.

A **GIANT** star can be 200 times as wide as the Sun and 1,000 times as bright.

A **SUPERGIANT** star can be 1,000 times as wide as the Sun and 10 million times as bright.

A **HYPERGIANT** star can be 2,100 times as wide as the Sun and up to 40 million times as bright. (Hypergiant stars last only a few million years.)

BIG RED

Betelgeuse is a red supergiant star that is 14,000 times brighter than the Sun and about 20 times as massive. If it were where the Sun is now, it would extend past Jupiter.

continued

The binary star system RS Ophiuchi contains a white dwarf star and a red giant star that orbit around each other.

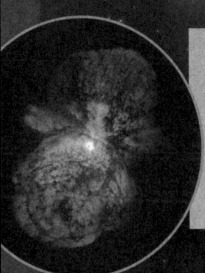

BIG BLUE

Hypergiant Eta Carinae is called a luminous blue variable (LBV) because it emits lots of energy, is extremely *hot*, and varies in brightness.

FADING STARS

★ **W**hen stars run out of fuel, they die. How this happens depends on their mass.

A WHITE DWARF is a small, dense, dying star that releases an expanding gas shell called a PLANETARY NEBULA. Stars the size of the Sun will eventually become white dwarfs.

Scientists think that white dwarfs become BLACK DWARFS. A black dwarf star emits no light. (There are no known black dwarfs in the universe.)

A large star can collapse in an explosion called a SUPERNOVA when it dies. (When a hypergiant does this, it's called a HYPERNOVA.) Gas and debris are violently ejected and the core of the star shrinks into a NEUTRON STAR.

Supernova 1987A in the Large Magellanic Cloud

A neutron star is small (6 to 12 miles wide) but dense: One teaspoonful of a neutron star would weigh as much as a small mountain on Earth. A neutron star spins very fast—as much as hundreds of times per second.

A PULSAR is a type of neutron star that emits energy in pulses, sort of like a light beam from a lighthouse.

When a massive star dies and collapses, it can form a STELLAR BLACK HOLE. The gravity of a black hole is so strong that it even pulls in light.

A supermassive black hole in Galaxy NGC 4438

★ A MID-MASS BLACK HOLE has a mass of hundreds to thousands of Suns.

★ A SUPERMASSIVE BLACK HOLE, with a mass millions to billions of times greater than that of the Sun, is thought to be at the center of most large galaxies.

SOMETHING Is EATING the MOON and SUN!

Myths and legends about eclipses abound. Before people understood the science of eclipses, they created stories to explain why the Moon or the Sun went dark. Many of the tales involved the death or downfall of a ruler or a great natural disaster. **Here are a few others**:

⬇ Ancient Egyptians believed that a mythical pig swallowed the Moon.

➡ According to Mayan folklore, a jaguar swallowed the Moon.

➡ In China, people believed that a three-leg toad devoured the Moon. During a solar eclipse, the Chinese would make a great noise and commotion—drumming, banging on pans, and shooting arrows into the sky—to restore daylight.

⬇ Today, in the Arctic, Eskimos, Aleuts, and Tlingits believe that an eclipse allows the Moon or Sun to leave the sky to see that things are all right on Earth.

SIZE WHYS

rom Earth, the Moon and the Sun appear to be about the same size, but their true sizes and locations make solar eclipses possible. The Moon can appear to cover the Sun (either totally or partially) because the diameter of the Sun is 400 times greater than that of the Moon, and the Sun is about 400 times farther away from Earth than the Moon is.

CONTINUED

HOW ECLIPSES HAPPEN

A TOTAL LUNAR ECLIPSE OCCURS WHEN . . .

Sun

Earth

MOON'S ORBIT

Earth passes directly between the Sun and the full Moon. The Moon passes through Earth's shadow and turns a coppery-red color. A lunar eclipse can last an hour or more.

A TOTAL SOLAR ECLIPSE OCCURS WHEN . . .

Sun

Earth

MOON'S ORBIT

the new Moon passes directly between the Sun and Earth, at just enough distance from Earth to completely block out the Sun. As the Moon obscures the sunlight, it casts a shadow (or path), some-times up to 200 miles wide, of semidarkness on Earth.

Why Totality Is Awesome

➡ You have to be in the shadow's path (and have clear skies) to see a total solar eclipse—and this is not always easy. The path often passes over open seas or remote regions.

➡ Local temperatures drop 20 degrees Fahrenheit or more near totality.

➡ Many animals and birds prepare for sleep or show confusion.

➡ Lunar eclipses can be seen from anywhere in the darkened hemisphere in which they occur, if skies are clear.

A S T R O N O M Y

Sky Watch Calendar

These total eclipses will be visible in North America

Total Lunar Eclipses

2010
December 21

2014
April 15
October 8

2015
April 4
September 28

Total Solar Eclipses

2017
August 21
PATH:............70 miles wide
ROUTE:.............Oregon to
South Carolina
TIME OF DAY:........mid-A.M. to
early P.M.
DURATION:...........almost 3
minutes

2024
April 8
PATH:...........120 miles wide
ROUTE:...............Texas to
New England
and eastern
Canada
TIME OF DAY: ......mid-A.M. to
mid-P.M.
DURATION: ....4.5 minutes

TRICK or TRADE?

In 1503, during his fourth voyage to the Americas, Christopher Columbus was stranded on the island of Jamaica. His ships were damaged, and he was running out of food. At first, he and his crew traded items from the ship for food from the natives. After a few months, the Jamaicans refused to supply any more food.

By early the next year, Columbus needed to do something to avoid starving. He studied his navigational tables and learned that a total eclipse of the Moon would occur on February 29, so he arranged a meeting with the natives for that night.

At the meeting, Columbus told the Jamaicans that he didn't like the way in which they were treating him and his crew. To show his displeasure, he said that he was going to take away the Moon. That very moment, Earth's shadow began to move across the face of the full Moon.

The natives were terrified! As the light of the Moon faded, they promised to give Columbus all the food he wanted if he would bring back the Moon.

Finally, certain that the Jamaicans would keep their promise—and moments before the end of the eclipse—Columbus announced that he would return the Moon to its place in the sky. The Moon reappeared and the grateful natives kept their part of the deal.

Columbus and his crew were eventually rescued, and they returned to Europe.

The Powers of ATTRACT

We live on a giant magnet. Earth's hard inner core contains iron that acts like a magnet, complete with magnetic north and south poles. These poles create a magnetic field around our planet that can attract and repel objects, even those that are far away.

(Have you ever noticed how a paper clip will jump to or push away from a magnet when placed near it? That's due to a magnetic field.) Earth's magnetic field helps us to find our way around. By using a compass, we can always find magnetic north.

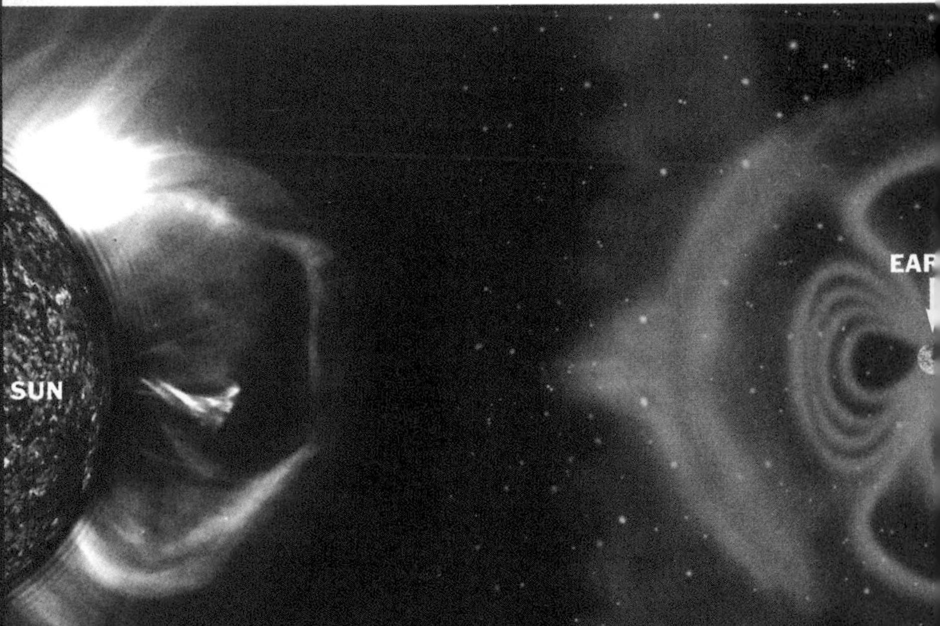

SUN

EAR

When massive solar explosions, or magnetic storms, occur, charged particles in the Sun's magnetic field race toward Earth at thousands of miles per second. Earth's magnetosphere, which extends outward about 40,000 miles on the Sun side, helps to protect us. However, intense magnetic storms can cause electric power outages on Earth.

Earth's outer core contains hot liquid iron that is constantly moving (think of boiling water). This causes Earth's magnetic field to increase or decrease and its magnetic poles to move. Earth's magnetic "north" pole travels about 25 miles per year. At that rate, it will be in Siberia in a few decades.

Sometimes a magnetic field completely reverses: Positive becomes negative and negative becomes positive. The last time this happened on Earth was about 780,000 years ago.

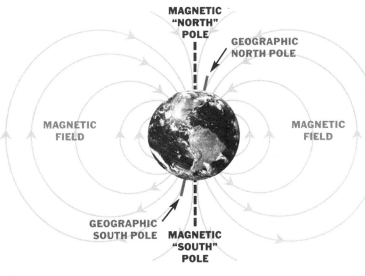

MAGNETIC
"NORTH"
POLE

GEOGRAPHIC
NORTH POLE

MAGNETIC
FIELD

MAGNETIC
FIELD

GEOGRAPHIC
SOUTH POLE

MAGNETIC
"SOUTH"
POLE

OPPOSING FORCES

➤ Earth's magnetic and geographic poles are not the same.

➤ What we call Earth's magnetic "north" pole is really a magnetic south pole. Because opposite poles attract, this pole draws the north pole of a magnetic compass needle toward it.

continued

A Stick-y Situation

Many **believe** that the magnet was discovered when a shepherd in the ancient Greek city of Magnesia put a piece of iron on the bottom of his walking stick so that it wouldn't wear out. He then noticed that certain stones stuck to the iron. These stones were called magnetite, after the city where they were found.

In the 11th century, scientists discovered that magnetite was a form of iron in rocks and that it could attract other rocks that contained iron. They also noticed that when a small, needle-shape piece of magnetite was suspended on a string or in water, the "needle" always pointed one way—north. (We now know that it pointed toward the Earth's magnetic "north" pole.) Travelers began to use magnetite needles as compasses. Eventually, people called magnetite the "leading stone" or "lodestone."

ALL IN THEIR HEADS

Some far-ranging animals, such as sea turtles and homing pigeons, are born with small amounts of magnetite in their brains. Scientists believe that the magnetite enables them to use Earth's magnetic field to "stay on course" during long trips.

HOLY COW!

Ever heard of a cow magnet? No, not a magnet in the shape of a cow. This is a magnet that is fed to a cow to attract pieces of barbed wire fence or other metal that the cow may have accidentally swallowed and that could injure its internal organs. To prevent the metal from circulating through the cow's body, the farmer inserts a magnet into the cow's mouth. When the cow swallows the magnet, it settles in its second stomach chamber—sometimes called the "hardware stomach"—where heavy eaten objects tend to collect. The magnet attracts any metal that the cow eats and usually remains in its stomach for the rest of its life.

Say, "Ahhhhh"

SUPER STAR

A **magnetar** is a rare type of neutron star with a magnetic field 1,000 trillion (1 quadrillion) times stronger than Earth's. Only about 12 have been found in the Milky Way and nearby galaxies. If Earth got close enough to a magnetar, the star could cause an aircraft carrier to spin around and point north more quickly than a compass needle moves on Earth today.

An artist's concept of what a magnetar might look like. The lines represent the star's superstrong magnetic field.

A Half Is as Good as a Whole

Magnets are usually made from iron, which, like everything else, is made of tiny particles called atoms. In many substances, the atoms are jumbled together (in no order), but the atoms in magnets all face in the same direction. If you cut a magnet in half, each piece will have a magnetic north and south pole—no matter how many halves you make!

these "attractive" experiments . . .

1

When a package says that the food inside is fortified with iron, it's true. Try this to see the iron in breakfast cereal.

YOU WILL NEED:

1 box high-iron-content cereal
mixing bowl
wood, plastic, or glass rod
tape
magnet (a light-color magnet works best)

→ Place about half of the cereal in a large bowl. Use your hands to crush the flakes into tiny pieces (pinhead size). Add enough water to make a soupy mixture. Tape a small magnet on the end of the rod and stir the cereal for several minutes. Remove the rod and magnet, and you will see tiny pieces of iron filings on the magnet.

2

Make an unmagnetized iron or steel object act like a magnet for a short period of time.

YOU WILL NEED:

bar magnet
nail
paper clip or thumbtack

→ Rub the bar magnet over the nail. Rub only in one direction, lifting the magnet when you reach the end of the nail. Do this about 40 times. (You are lining up the atoms in the nail to face in the same direction.) See if the nail will attract the paper clip or thumbtack.

FAR OUT!

How can I tell if I am seeing a star or a planet?

A: **The twinkle.** Stars twinkle and planets usually do not, although one might appear to twinkle if Earth's atmosphere is turbulent. To check, watch the object over several nights to see if it moves across the sky. If it moves, chances are it's a planet.

The word "planet" comes from the Greek word for "wanderer."

Do all planets rotate, or spin?

A: **Yes, but at different rates.** Jupiter spins the fastest. One day on Jupiter equals 10 hours on Earth. Venus turns the slowest. One day there equals about 243 days on Earth. Why planets rotate is a mystery, but because there is no friction in space, the spinning can continue forever or slow due to forces from other objects, such as a moon, planet, or star. Earth's rotation is slowing about 2 seconds every 100,000 years because of the Moon's tidal forces and other effects. Can you feel it?

The Sun spins. Its equator complete one rotation every 25 Earth days. The Sun's poles spin more slowly because it is a gaseous not solid, body.

What is the International Space Station?

A: Home, to space pioneers. The International Space Station, or ISS, is a cooperative effort of 16 nations that serves as a laboratory for experiments in communications, health, biology, physics, technology, and more. Started in 1998, it is scheduled to be complete in 2010. At that time, it will be about the length of a football field. Its international crews live on it for 6 months at a time, in about 15,000 cubic feet of living space (more than in a typical three-bedroom house). Orbiting 240 miles above Earth, the ISS circles the planet about every 90 minutes. To find out when you can see the ISS in your area, go to: www.jsc.nasa.gov/sightings.

The International Space Station is powered by solar energy.

GIANT JUPITER *and*

Jupiter and its four planet-size moons, called the Galilean Satellites. Photographed by *Voyager 1* and assembled into this collage by NASA's Jet Propulsion Laboratory, they are shown in their relative positions, though not to scale.

Galileo

JUPITER, the fifth planet out from the Sun, is the largest planet in our solar system. With four planet-size moons and at least 59 smaller ones, Jupiter would have its own miniature solar system if it were a star.

On January 7, 1610, using a very primitive telescope, astronomer Galileo Galilei saw three small "stars" near Jupiter. About a week later, a fourth "star" appeared. (These were actually Jupiter's four largest moons.) At about the same time, a German astronomer, Simon Marius, also claimed to have seen the moons. But Simon did not publish his observations, so Galileo gets the credit. Today, these moons are called Io, Europa, Ganymede, and Callisto, and they are what is known as the Galilean Satellites.

ts MANY MOONS

Earth   Jupiter

Jupiter is about 11 times larger than Earth. Its core temperature may reach as high as 50,000°F.

Jupiter's turbulent atmosphere moves in bands around the planet (see it at Almanac4kids.com/jupiter). Lightning strikes and storms as big as hurricanes on Earth are common.

The Great Red Spot is a storm that is three times the size of Earth and has winds of up to 250 mph. It has been raging in Jupiter's atmosphere for at least 300 years.

OVER THE MOONS

IO *The Pizza Moon*

Think of a giant pizza, with melted cheese, tomato sauce, and ripe olives. That's what Io, the most volcanically active body in the solar system, looks like. "Toppings" on the surface are actually sulfur in different colorful forms. Jupiter's strong gravity causes 300-foot-high "tides" in Io's solid surface. (The difference between the lowest and highest ocean tides on Earth is "only" about 60 feet!)

continued

EUROPA
The Ocean Moon

Think of Earth's South Pole, a frozen mass with an ocean underneath. That's Europa. Under an icy crust, Europa may have oceans as deep as 30 miles or more. Altogether, Europa is believed to have twice as much water as Earth.

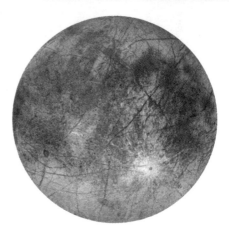

GANYMEDE
The Rocky Moon

Think of a huge, magnetic rock. With a diameter of 3,280 miles, Ganymede has mountains, valleys, craters, and lava flows covered with rock and ice, plus its own magnetic field. Ganymede is Jupiter's largest moon and the largest in our solar system. If it orbited the Sun instead of Jupiter, it would be a planet.

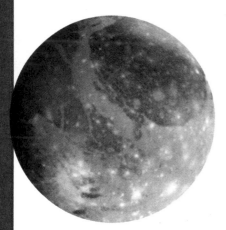

CALLISTO
The Oldest Moon

Think of a dimpled golf ball. That's Callisto. About 4 billion years old, Callisto has the oldest landscape in the solar system, the most craters, and no volcanic activity.

ASTEROIDS, BY JOVE!

➡️ **Some of Jupiter's numerous small moons might be asteroids captured by the giant planet's gravity.**

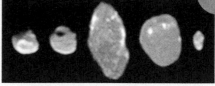

These images of the small inner moons of Jupiter, taken during *Galileo*'s 11th orbit around the Giant Planet in November 1997, are the best available.

DID YOU KNOW?

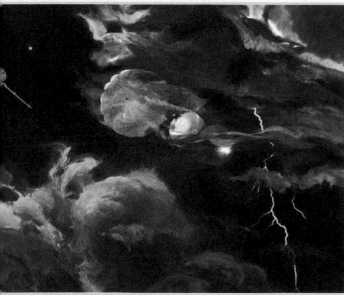

Jupiter is named for the king of the Roman gods, who was also known as Jove.

One year on Jupiter is equal to nearly 12 years on Earth.

Because of Jupiter's strong gravity, if you weigh 100 pounds on Earth you would weigh 240 pounds on Jupiter!

⬆️ NASA's *Galileo* spacecraft reached Jupiter in 1995, after traveling for 6 years. Above is an artist's depiction of the *Galileo* probe descending into Jupiter's violent atmosphere. During its 58-minute life, the probe measured temperature, pressure, chemical composition, cloud characteristics, sunlight and energy, and lightning before it was crushed and/or vaporized by the pressure and temperature of the atmosphere.

In 2011, NASA's Jupiter Polar Orbiter *(Juno)* will leave Earth and fly to Jupiter to orbit its polar regions and learn about the planet's size and structure, atmosphere, temperature, and winds. *Juno* is expected to reach Jupiter in 2016.

RS!

"Tornado" comes from the Spanish word *tronada,* meaning "thunderstorm," which was used in the 14th century by sailors for a violent, windy thunderstorm.

A tornado is a violently rotating column of air between a storm cloud and Earth, touching both suddenly and with little or no warning. This column can be more than 50,000 feet high. When conditions are right, a thunderstorm can spin out one or more tornadoes. Any tornado can vary greatly in length, width, direction of travel, and speed.

continued

44

The United States has the highest incidence of tornadoes, or twisters, in the world—about 1,000 every year. Although tornadoes have occurred in all 50 states, Tornado Alley (an area covering all or parts of Arkansas, Iowa, Kansas, Louisiana, Minnesota, Nebraska, North Dakota, Ohio, Oklahoma, South Dakota, and Texas) experiences them most frequently. This is due to cold polar air from Canada, warm tropical air from the Gulf of Mexico, and dry air from the Southwest clashing in the middle of the country.

Tornadoes occur on every continent except Antarctica.

HOW A TORNADO FORMS

Rising warm air creates updraft

Downdraft

Differing wind speeds and directions cause air to roll horizontally

A thunderstorm forms when warm, moist air collides with cool, dry air. Winds traveling at different speeds and in different directions create a horizontally rolling column of air. Rising warm air creates an updraft that lifts the horizontal air until it is vertical. Nearby descending air, called a downdraft, pulls the rotating column to the ground. When impact is made, the downdraft spreads out and circulates back up, causing the rotation to increase dramatically and sometimes create a tornado.

➤ DEADLIEST TORNADO

On March 18, 1925, the Tri-State Tornado raced along at 60 to 73 miles per hour in a 219-mile-long track across parts of Missouri, Illinois, and Indiana. It killed 695 people.

Typical residential scenes in Murphysboro, Illinois, where 154 city blocks were destroyed and about half of the population died.

➤ WIDEST TORNADO

On May 22, 2004, a nearly 2½-mile-wide tornado struck Hallam, Nebraska.

WEATHER

HOW TORNADOES ARE MEASURED

The Fujita Scale (or F Scale) was developed by Dr. Theodore Fujita to classify tornadoes and severe windstorms and assign them a number based on wind damage. An enhanced F scale (EF) was implemented in the United States on February 1, 2007.

F SCALE		EF SCALE (U.S.)
F0 • 40–72 mph (64–116 km/h)	light damage	EF0 • 65–85 mph (105–137 km/h)
F1 • 73–112 mph (117–180 km/h)	moderate damage	EF1 • 86–110 mph (138–178 km/h)
F2 • 113–157 mph (181–253 km/h)	considerable damage	EF2 • 111–135 mph (179–218 km/h)
F3 • 158–207 mph (254–332 km/h)	severe damage	EF3 • 136–165 mph (219–266 km/h)
F4 • 208–260 mph (333–419 km/h)	devastating damage	EF4 • 166–200 mph (267–322 km/h)
F5 • 261–318 mph (420–512 km/h)	incredible damage	EF5 • over 200 mph (over 322 km/h)

➤ MOST CREATIVE FAKE TORNADO

The tornado in the movie *The Wizard of Oz* was simulated by using a 35-foot muslin stocking attached to a crane and rotating motor. The dust and thick clouds were created using Fuller's earth (claylike soil), carbon, and sulfur.

➤ MOST TORNADOES

On April 3 and 4, 1974, 148 tornadoes touched down in a total of 13 U.S. states.

➤ HIGHEST NUMBER OF HITS

Oklahoma City has been hit by more than 100 tornadoes.

continued

Why People Still Talk About TUPELO

On April 5, 1936, when Elvis Presley was almost a year and a half old, a tornado swept through his hometown of Tupelo, Mississippi. The storm destroyed homes across the street from the Presley house (they escaped unharmed); killed 216 people; blew a kitchen, intact, to the town of Mooresville, 7 miles away; and sucked feathers off of chickens.

Elvis Presley in 1937 with his parents, Gladys and Vernon Presley.

DID YOU KNOW?

➤ A dust devil can form over irrigated fields.

➤ A funnel cloud doesn't touch the ground.

➤ A waterspout forms over warm water and can move onshore.

A pale green sky means the wind is high.

–proverb

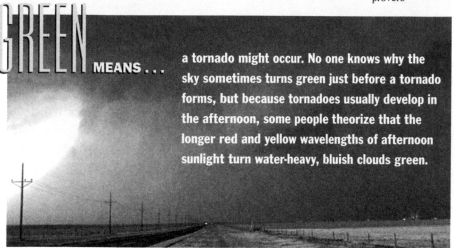

GREEN MEANS . . .

a tornado might occur. No one knows why the sky sometimes turns green just before a tornado forms, but because tornadoes usually develop in the afternoon, some people theorize that the longer red and yellow wavelengths of afternoon sunlight turn water-heavy, bluish clouds green.

WAYS TO STAY SAFE

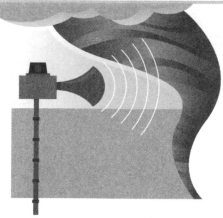

• A **TORNADO WATCH** indicates possible tornadoes in your area. Stay tuned to the radio or television news.

• A **TORNADO WARNING** means that a tornado is on the ground or has been detected by Doppler radar. Seek shelter immediately!

➤ **IF YOU ARE INDOORS,** take cover in the cellar or a small space (a closet or bathroom) in the interior of your home. Stay away from windows!

➤ **IF YOU ARE OUTDOORS,** find a field or ditch away from items that can fly through the air and lie down as flat as you can.

➤ **DO NOT STAY IN A CAR** or try to drive away from a tornado. Cars can be flung about by high winds or crushed by debris.

MAKE A WIND CHIME

Catch the

Tools are available to catch the speed of the wind (an anemometer) and the direction of the wind (a wind sock or wind vane). A wind chime makes music from the wind.

Wind chimes come in many sizes and shapes. Your wind chime's sound will depend on what you use. Experiment with a variety of materials or use several at once. Try . . .

- metal spoons and forks, other old silverware
- bamboo or other wood
- metal washers
- old keys
- seashells
- soda cans (empty and rinsed)
- plastic balls
- bells
- scratched or unwanted CDs

YOU WILL NEED:

- a hanger, such as a coat hanger, wooden dowel, or stick

- string, yarn, or fishing line

- scissors

- three or more "chimes" (the heavier the chime, the stronger the wind needed to move it)

- a drill or other tool to pierce a hole in the chimes for the string

- decorating materials (paint, glue, sparkles, ribbon, markers, etc.)

1 Gather materials.

2 Decorate the chimes, if desired.

3 If necessary, drill a hanging hole into the chimes. (Ask an adult for help.) Tie or glue a piece of string to each chime. Experiment with using different lengths of string.

Wind

Every wind has its weather. —Francis Bacon, English philosopher (1561–1626)

4 Arrange the chimes by tying them to the hanger. Heavier objects should be in the center, for balance. Attach them loosely until you are sure that the arrangement balances and sounds good. Make sure that the chimes will touch when they are moved by the wind. Rearrange as needed.

5 Find a breezy place to hang your creation.

➤ Wind chimes can also be called aeolian chimes. Aeolus was the ruler of the wind in Greek mythology.

➤ In Japan, wind chimes are hung in the corners of Buddhist temples, where hearing them is said to bring good luck.

Top 10 Windiest Places in the United States

1 Mount Washington, New Hampshire
2 St. Paul Island, Alaska
3 Cold Bay, Alaska
4 Blue Hill, Massachusetts
5 Dodge City, Kansas
6 Amarillo, Texas
7 Barter Island, Alaska
8 Cheyenne, Wyoming
9 Kahului, Hawaii
10 Rochester, Minnesota

–National Oceanic and Atmospheric Administration (NOAA)

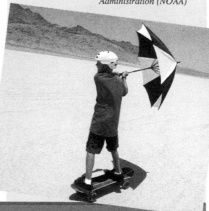

Top 10 Windiest Places in Canada

1 St. John's, Newfoundland
2 Gander, Newfoundland
3 Summerside, Prince Edward Island
4 Swift Current, Saskatchewan
5 Regina, Saskatchewan
6 Sydney, Nova Scotia
7 Estevan, Saskatchewan
8 Lethbridge, Alberta
9 Moose Jaw, Saskatchewan
10 Charlottetown, Prince Edward Island

–Environment Canada

CLOUDY, WITH A Chance of FISH

No one has ever seen it rain cats and dogs—

but some people have seen it rain fish and frogs.

IT'S RAINING FISH . . .

On the afternoon of May 15, 1900, the sky over Olneyville, Rhode Island, became nearly as dark as night, the temperature dropped more than 20 degrees in just a few minutes, and lightning crackled. Suddenly, the clouds opened up and dumped rain—and fish—on the town. Most of the fish were 2- to 4-inch-long pout, but residents of some neighborhoods reported being pelted with perch. Children scooped up fish to sell as souvenirs. Some adults wouldn't go near the fish because they believed that the unusual rainfall was a sign of impending doom. Many families saved at least one fish to display, and a local restaurant showed off one in a tank of water.

. . . AND FROGS

Amid the high winds and rain of Hurricane Isabel in September 2003, a man in Berlin, Connecticut, discovered that tiny, gooey eggs with a dark spot in the middle had landed on his porch. He thought that they were probably frogs' eggs, and he was right. He brought them inside and kept them in a bowl of water, and, within a few days, they began sprouting tails—the beginnings of pollywogs.

Because September is too late in the season (and too cold) for frogs to lay their eggs in Connecticut, it is believed that the eggs were picked up in a warmer, more southern state, such as North Carolina, and carried north on the winds of the hurricane.

(continued)

FISH Out of WATER

When a severe storm with very strong winds, such as a thunderstorm or tornado, passes over a lake or ocean, it may scoop up fish or frogs that are near the surface. If the wind is strong enough, it can carry the creatures for many miles (sometimes hundreds) before the storm clouds burst and "rain out" the fish or frogs.

LOOK OUT, BELOW!

RED "BLOOD" RAINS are caused by reddish sand from the Sahara Desert that is carried by winds traveling north or west across the Atlantic. When it rains, the red dust in the clouds falls to the ground as "bloody" red drops.

For two days in 2002, a town in Sangrampur, India, experienced **GREEN RAIN.** A pollution scientist discovered that the specks were fecal droppings from giant Asian honeybees that had just fed on pollen from local mangoes and coconuts.

RED RAINS can also occur under clear skies. When certain young butterflies, including monarchs, emerge from their cocoons and take their first flights, they eject a red liquid that is really poop. Objects below become speckled with bloodlike markings.

WEIRD AND WEIRDER "WEATHER"

1873 **FROGS** rained on Kansas City, Missouri.

1877 Live, footlong **ALLIGATORS** landed on a farm in South Carolina.

1881 **PERIWINKLES** and **HERMIT CRABS** showered residents of Worcester, England.

1948 **HERRING** pelted golfers in Bournemouth, England.

1981 **FROGS** that were later determined to be a species that was native to North Africa fell on Naphilion, Greece.

2000 **SMALL FISH** —dead, but still fresh—rained over Great Yarmouth, England.

2001 **DRIED CORNHUSKS** fell over an area in east Wichita, Kansas.

not-so-fishy forecasts

• When fish jump up after flies, expect rain.
• The louder the frogs, the more the rain.

For more proverbs and the weather where you are, go to Almanac4kids.com/weather.

THE CHILLING TALE OF THE

Using paper flakes and a pointer instead of a broom straw, Wilson "Snowflake" Bentley demonstrated how he moved a snowflake from the tray to the slide of his microscope.

Wilson Bentley was born in 1865 and raised on a farm near Jericho, Vermont, where his mother, a former teacher, homeschooled him and his brother when they weren't doing farm chores. When Willie turned 15, his mother gave him the best birthday present he ever got—her old microscope. Through the lens, he studied drops of water, bird feathers, and flower petals, but most of all he loved to look at snowflakes. He spent hours examining and trying to draw snowflakes, holding his breath so that they wouldn't melt—which they often did.

When he was 17, Willie asked his parents to buy him a new, better microscope and a camera. His father argued that "fussing with snowflakes" was a waste of time. Finally, he gave in.

Willie built a wooden frame to hold the new equipment and then spent 2 years figuring out how to take a picture of a snowflake under a microscope. On January 15, 1885, he did it, creating the world's first photomicrograph (photograph of a microscope image).

Every winter for the rest of his life, Willie photographed and studied snowflakes in an unheated room in the back of the house. The process was extremely difficult and cold! Outdoors, he collected snowflakes on a wooden tray that was painted black. Once inside, while still wearing big mittens to keep his hands warm, he used a straw plucked from a broom to pick up the snowflake and place it on a microscope slide. Sometimes he nudged the

SNOWFLAKE MAN

snowflake into place with a feather. Then, being careful not to breathe on the flake, he quickly examined and photographed it.

Whenever it snowed, Willie caught and captured flakes, sometimes working all night. He found that most snowflakes had six sides, but others looked like triangles, spools of thread, or columns. If he used his imagination, he could see that some flakes resembled objects: flowers, birds, even milk bottles. Some were plain, others were lacy—but no two were alike.

If snowflakes increase in size, a thaw will follow.

—proverb

(continued)

When the snow falls dry,

it means to lie;

But flakes light and soft

will bring rain oft.

–proverb

Taking photomicrographs was only half of a long process. In those days, glass plates were used to take photographs. Willie developed the plates in a darkroom under some stairs and then carried the plates to a nearby stream to wash them. Sometimes he did this at night, in the dark.

In warm months, Willie presented outdoor slide shows about snowflakes to family and friends. He shined a kerosene lamp through a projector that held his glass plates. The lamplight cast the snowflake images onto a bedsheet hung up to serve as a screen. "The mysteries of the universe are about to reveal themselves," he would say. "Look and marvel."

Willie shared his snowflakes with anyone who was interested. He sold prints of his photomicrographs for 5 cents each. He wrote articles for scientists and for magazines such as *National Geographic*. Occasionally, he felt discouraged that few people seemed to care about his work. Still, he never stopped. At age 65, he photographed his 5,000th snowflake.

Slowly, people became interested. Reporters sometimes appeared at his door. People began to call him "the Snowflake Man" and "Professor Bentley." Jewelry makers copied the snowflake designs. In 1920, the American Meteorological Society elected him as one of its first members and gave him their first research grant. Although Willie did travel to lecture about snowflakes, he seldom did so in winter, not wanting to miss a research opportunity. As he once explained,

"A snowstorm is always so exciting to me. I never know when I am going to find some wonderful prize."

Willie's proudest moment came in 1931 upon publication of his book *Snow Crystals,* which contained 2,453 of his photographs. A few weeks later, on December 7, he wrote in his weather notebook: "Cold north wind afternoon. Snow flying." This was to be his last entry. He became sick, and died of pneumonia on December 23.

The next day, the *Burlington Free Press,* a Vermont newspaper, published a long editorial saluting Wilson "Snowflake" Bentley. It reads: "Bentley was a living example of . . . genius. He saw something in the snowflakes that other men failed to see, not because they could not see, but because they had not the patience and the understanding to look."

A RARE PAIR

The long-held belief that no two snowflakes are alike was shattered by Nancy Knight, a cloud physicist with the National Center for Atmospheric Research in Boulder, Colorado, in 1988. While on a flight over Wausau, Wisconsin, she collected snowflakes on an oil-coated piece of glass hanging beneath the plane. Later, while studying photographs of her catch, she discovered the two identical, columnar snowflakes, attached to each other. For years, she kept the pair in a freezer in her laboratory.

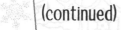 (continued)

A GUIDE TO SNOWFLAKES

If you look closely at snowflakes, you will see many different shapes.
Here are some of the most common ones.

simple prism	solid column	sheath	scroll on plate	triangular
hexagonal plate	hollow column	cup	column on plate	12-branched star
stellar plate	bullet rosette	capped column	split plate and star	radiating plates
sectored plate	isolated bullet	multiple capped columns	skeletal	radiating dendrite
simple star	simple needle	capped bullets	twin columns	irregulars
stellar dendrite	needle clusters	double plates	arrowhead twins	rimed
fernlike stellar dendrite	crossed needles	hollow plate	crossed plates	graupel

Let It Snow!

No matter what the weather looks like outside, it can be winter where you are. Paper snowflakes are especially fun to make and hang during the end-of-year holidays.

YOU WILL NEED:

- square pieces of white paper*
- scissors
- string or thread
- tape

1 Fold the paper in half diagonally.

FOLD

2 Fold the triangle in half . . .

FOLD

3 . . . then fold one third to the front and one third to the back.

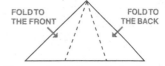

FOLD TO THE FRONT   FOLD TO THE BACK

4 Trim the points off the bottom.

5 Cut into the folds.

Experiment by making different shapes, sizes, and numbers of cuts. Be sure not to cut all the way across the triangle.

6 Carefully unfold your creation. Cut a length of string. Tape one end to the edge of the flake and the other end to the ceiling or a window.

*If you are cutting standard 8½ x11-inch paper to make it square, save the ends. Try making baby flakes with them or use the paper for notes.

Q: What do snowmen eat for breakfast?

A: Snowflakes

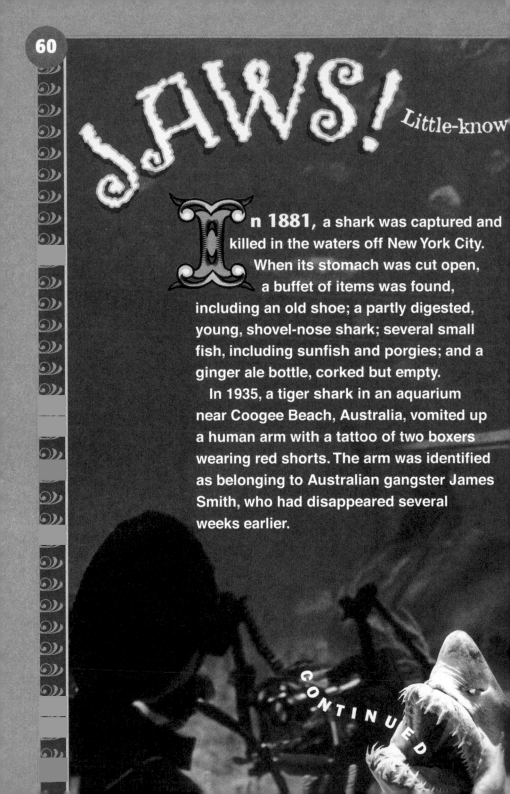

JAWS! Little-know

In 1881, a shark was captured and killed in the waters off New York City. When its stomach was cut open, a buffet of items was found, including an old shoe; a partly digested, young, shovel-nose shark; several small fish, including sunfish and porgies; and a ginger ale bottle, corked but empty.

In 1935, a tiger shark in an aquarium near Coogee Beach, Australia, vomited up a human arm with a tattoo of two boxers wearing red shorts. The arm was identified as belonging to Australian gangster James Smith, who had disappeared several weeks earlier.

CONTINUED

...d hard-to-swallow facts about SHARKS

A lemon shark

Detectives discovered that one of James's partners in crime had cut his body into pieces and thrown them into the ocean. It is believed that a baby shark ate James's arm, but before it was able to digest it, the young shark was eaten by a tiger shark, which was captured soon after and brought to the aquarium.

A tiger shark

These items have been found in the stomachs of sharks:

- a man's wallet
- 25 bottles of water (1 quart each) bound together with a wire hoop
- a nearly whole reindeer
- 6 horseshoe crabs
- 3 bottles of beer
- a blue penguin
- a handbag containing 3 shillings
- a belt
- a wristwatch
- a full-grown spaniel
- a yellow-billed cuckoo

Tiger sharks may be the most gluttonous of all sharks. They have been known to try to digest beer bottles, bags of potatoes, coal, dogs, overcoats, a driver's license, a cow's hoof, the antlers of a deer, and a chicken coop with feathers and bones still inside. Fortunately for them, tiger sharks have a kind of safety valve if they eat too much junk food. They throw up.

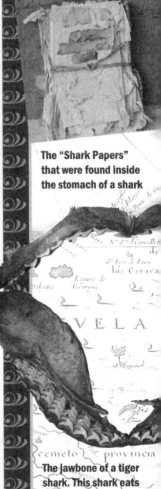

The "Shark Papers" that were found inside the stomach of a shark

The jawbone of a tiger shark. This shark eats almost anything and is the most dangerous of all species of fish.

FISH CATCHES MAN

In August 1799, an American ship named *Nancy* was sailing in the Caribbean Sea, captained by Thomas Briggs. All was well until the captain of the H.M.S. *Sparrow*, a British ship, seized the *Nancy* because he believed that Thomas was smuggling goods between Aruba, an island near Venezuela, and the United States.

Thomas claimed that he was innocent, but he was arrested and a trial was scheduled in Kingston, Jamaica. Because the lawyers had little evidence to prove that he had been smuggling, Thomas was confident that he would be freed of all charges.

During the trial, a British merchant ship arrived in Jamaica. Its captain claimed to have proof that Thomas was guilty. While at sea, the British crew had caught a shark; inside its stomach, they had found papers with details about smuggling that Thomas had written!

No longer able to lie, Thomas confessed that before he was captured, he had thrown the papers overboard. He was angry that he had been caught by a "bloody shark fish."

The documents became known as the "Shark Papers" and are on exhibit at the Institute of Jamaica. For a while, the shark's jaw was on display near the courthouse at the corner of Harbour and Hanover streets in Kingston as a reminder that honesty is the best policy. The jaw is now also at the Institute of Jamaica.

CONTINUED

What is a shark's favorite kind of sandwich?

A: Peanut butter and jellyfish!

A great white shark

Remora fish hitch a ride on the dorsal fin of a lemon shark.

See what some kids (and teachers!) are doing to save sharks at www.sharks.org/education_kids.htm.

SHARK MARKS

- Although the use of shark body parts as food and in products is diminishing in much of the world, shark fin is still used to make soup and shark meat continues to be eaten.

- Shark skin was once a popular alternative to leather.

- Shark liver oil was once used as an ingredient in cosmetics, as a salve to help wounds heal, as a source of Vitamin A, as a protective coating on wooden boats, and as street-lamp fuel.

- Shark body parts are used as ingredients in some tanning oils and glues.

- Shark teeth are used in jewelry and ceremonial objects.

They Dare to Care

Remoras (shown at left) and pilot fish are often found hanging out with sharks, which serve as 24/7 "bodyguards" for the smaller fish.

Remoras attach themselves to a shark and help to keep it clean by eating parasites, lice, small crabs, and other critters that live on its skin. Sometimes, remoras will cling to the inside of a shark's mouth (never in its stomach) and remove bits of food between the shark's teeth. Occasionally, a remora will leave the shark for a while to feast on scraps of food that the shark has left floating around. It then swims back and reattaches itself to the shark.

Pilot fish swim ahead of and alongside a shark and feast on scraps released as the shark feeds. It is unclear why sharks don't eat pilot fish.

Beating the HEAT

Animals that live in the desert have special ways of coping with the extreme heat and dryness of their environment. Here are a few and what they do:

GO BELOW: Gila monsters, tarantulas, and desert tortoises make their homes under the sand or soil, where it is cooler. **Kangaroo rats** seal off their tunnels during the day to prevent heat from entering and keep the humid air inside from escaping.

SLEEP THROUGH IT: Round-tailed ground squirrels, spadefoot toads, and desert tortoises go into a sleep similar to hibernation called "estivation."

TIME IT RIGHT: Bats, owls, and many rodents sleep in shady shelters during the day and come

GILA MONSTER

BOBCAT

DESERT TORTOISE

out at night, when it's cooler. **Kit foxes, coyotes,** and **bobcats** tend to be active between dusk and dawn.

USE THEIR EARS: Jackrabbits and **mule deer** have big ears with lots of blood vessels. As blood travels through the ears' arteries and veins, it radiates heat out, which helps the animals to cool down.

GO LIGHT: Desert iguanas have cream-color skin that reflects heat, helping them to be comfortable in their hot, sandy home.

RUN FOR COVER: Zebra-tailed **lizards** and a few others run quickly over hot spots to reach the shade.

Some lizards, such as **collared lizards** and **Mojave fringe-toed lizards,** travel on two legs, rather than all four, for short distances. Snakes called **sidewinders** travel in such a way that only a small part of their body touches the scorching sand at any one time.

EVAPORATE: Turkey vultures cool down by urinating on their legs. The liquid cools them as it evaporates. Some **tortoises** drool to cool their necks and front legs. **Owls** pant and vibrate the throat (called "gular fluttering") to evaporate moisture in their mouths and throats.

CONTINUED

JACKRABBIT

DESERT IGUANA

ZEBRA-TAILED LIZARD

SIDEWINDER

HOW HOT?

DEATH VALLEY, in the southern California portion of the Mojave Desert, is the hottest place in North America. Its highest temperature, 134°F, was recorded on July 10, 1913.

THE SONORAN DESERT, which covers parts of southeastern California, southwestern Arizona, Baja California, and Mexico's state of Sonora, has the most diverse mix of plants and animals of any desert in North America. Temperatures there can exceed 120°F in summer.

FLY HIGH: Eagles, **hawks,** and **vultures** soar high in the sky, where the air is cooler.

TURN THEIR BACKS: The **antelope ground squirrel** and others stand with their backs to the Sun and shade their bodies with their tails.

CONSERVE: Desert **bighorn sheep** store several days' worth of water in their bodies. To conserve water, birds, insects, and reptiles such as **snakes** excrete gooey uric acid instead of liquid urine.

REUSE: **Gila monsters** and **desert tortoises** have large bladders that hold lots of water, which can be reabsorbed when needed. **Roadrunners** recycle water from the lower intestine.

MAKE DO: As **kangaroo rats** digest dry seeds, their bodies make water to help them to survive.

GO AWAY: **Pronghorn antelope** migrate to the mountains or other cooler areas when the desert is hottest.

DESERT BIGHORN SHEEP

ROADRUNN

ANTELOPE GROUND SQUIRREL

Food for the BIRD FEEDER

BIRD	Sunflower seeds	Millet	Thistle seeds	Safflower seeds	Cracked corn	Peanuts	Peanut butter	Suet	Raisins	Apples	Oranges and grapefruit
Cardinal	✓	✓		✓	✓				✓	✓	✓
Chickadee	✓	✓	✓	✓	✓	✓	✓	✓			
Finch	✓	✓	✓	✓	✓	✓	✓				✓
Goldfinch	✓		✓								
Junco	✓	✓	✓	✓	✓						
Nuthatch	✓	✓				✓	✓	✓			
Sparrow	✓	✓		✓	✓	✓					
Titmouse	✓	✓		✓	✓	✓	✓	✓			
Woodpecker						✓	✓	✓			

TRASH TALK

● **TRASH, GARBAGE, WASTE.** Whatever its name, there's lots of it.

More than 251 million tons of municipal solid waste— or trash—was produced in the United States in 2006. This means that, on average, each American produced about 4.6 pounds of waste per day.

Where does it all go? Much goes to landfills. Some is incinerated. A lot is recycled . . . but what does this mean?

CANS

● More than 120,000 ALUMINUM CANS are recycled every minute in the United States. Here's how:

Cans placed in recycling containers are sent to large scrap-processing companies. There, machines crush cans into 30-pound bricks.

Aluminum companies take the bricks, shred and crush them, and burn off any logos or decorations.

Potato chip–size pieces of this aluminum are placed in melting furnaces, where they are blended with new aluminum.

This blended aluminum is poured into 25-foot-long molds to make bars that weigh over 30,000 pounds. The bars are fed into machines that reduce the metal thickness from 20 inches or more down to about $\frac{1}{100}$ of an inch thick.

This metal is then coiled and ready to go to a can-making company that will deliver new cans to beverage companies.

PAPER

● Most landfills contain more **PAPER** than anything else—about 40 percent, on average. Compacted paper doesn't deteriorate well. Newspapers from the 1960s are still legible!

CONTINUED

CARS

● **ABOUT 27 MILLION CARS AROUND THE WORLD** stop working and are recycled each year. Almost 80 percent of car components are recycled. The remaining 20 percent is called "auto shredder residue," most of which goes into landfills each year.

At least 275 million scrap tires are stockpiled in the United States. About 80 percent of these are sold for various uses:

- ✹ new tires
- ✹ floor mats
- ✹ tire-derived fuel
- ✹ shoe soles
- ✹ rubberized asphalt
- ✹ boat bumpers

GREEN
BOTTLES & JARS
ONLY

GLASS

● **GLASS**–juice and soda bottles, food jars, and the like–is easily recyclable.

■ Glass containers are crushed into "cullet."

■ Cullet is mixed with sand, soda ash, and limestone.

■ The mixture is heated to between 2,600° and 2,800°F and poured into molds to make new glass containers.

About 90 percent of recycled glass is used to make new containers.

PLASTIC

- PLASTIC IS HANDY—and everywhere. Most plastic is not biodegradable and not recycled, and this is a problem. The "Great Pacific Garbage Patch" is a large area of the Pacific Ocean where currents cause debris (80 percent of it plastic) to accumulate and drift, sometimes for a decade or more. Ocean life gets tangled in plastic nets, while some species eat plastic items, which are toxic. Sometimes beaches in Hawaii get coated with blue-green plastic "sand," too. Plastic debris can wash up virtually anywhere.

Some 500 billion to 1 trillion plastic bags are used around the world each year.

CONTINUED

DID YOU KNOW?

- Many **CELL PHONES, COMPUTERS,** and TVs contain lead and mercury, which are harmful and should not be put into landfills. Electronics should be "e-cycled" (donated to a place that can use them or dropped off at a certified e-recycler).

ZAP, FLASH, GONE!

- **PLASMA GASIFICATION is** a waste treatment technology that uses electricity and very high temperatures to break down waste.

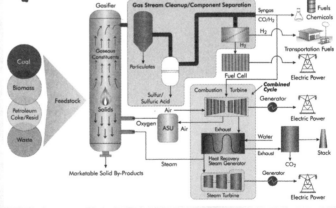

An example of how gasification works

It can reduce one ton of trash down to 5 cubic feet in less than a minute. It can vaporize a pair of old sneakers into something resembling a small glass bead—which can be used for road construction fill—while creating gases that can be used to make alternative fuel.

ROT RATE

The time required to decompose...

Paper . . . . 2.5 months

Orange peel . . . . 6 months

Wax-coated milk
carton . . . . 5 years

Plastic bag . . . . 10 to 20 years

Disposable diaper . . . 75 years

Tin can . . . . 100 years

Styrofoam . . . . never

Trash Through Time

- Ever wonder what people from the past did with trash? Have a look at the messy subject through the ages at "Rotten Truth (About Garbage)," www.astc.org/exhibitions/rotten/timeline.htm.

CONTINUED

TOMORROWLANDS

An artist's depiction of Masdar City. It will hold 50,000 people and 1,500 businesses.

● The world's first zero-carbon city will be **MASDAR CITY** in the **UNITED ARAB EMIRATES.** Its energy sources will be the Sun (82 percent); composted food waste, which is burned (17 percent); and wind (1 percent). People will travel by foot or by light rail or small pods powered by photovoltaic panels.

● **CHINA** plans to build an "eco city" on an island. **DONGTAN** will capture and purify water; have special recycling, heat, and power systems; and allow no cars.

TRASH TO CASH

Proof that one man's trash really is another man's treasure:

► New York City artist Justin Gignac fills plastic cubes with things that he picks up on the streets, such as theater tickets, subway passes, newspapers, and snack bags. Then he signs, numbers, dates, and sells each cube as "NYC Garbage." Some cubes have themes. One is trash from an opening-day baseball game at Yankee Stadium.

► German artist HA Schult makes life-size "Trash People" out of rubbish. Though he creates his "people" using many items of trash, he sometimes makes the faces out of tin cans, the chests from computers, and the arms and legs from crushed plastic—all to remind everyone of the waste they produce. Schult has been exhibiting Trash People around the world since 1996.

◄ Boris Bally of Providence, Rhode Island, creates tables, chairs, jewelry, and bowls from old metal traffic signs. He scours huge scrap piles for just the right pieces of metal. His work has been shown in museums around the world.

● What do you do to reuse or recycle trash? Share your ideas at Almanac4kids.com/tellus.

THE SEARCH IS ON FO[

The gasoline that powers most cars, lawn mowers, boats, and other machines is produced from oil, a **FOSSIL FUEL** made from long-dead sea plants and animals. It takes at least 10 million years for these remains to turn into crude oil, and we just can't wait that long, so scientists are exploring alternatives to oil for creating energy.

WAYS TO GO!

Fill 'er Up, With Food?

OF PARTICULAR INTEREST to scientists are biofuels, which are derived from recently living matter such as corn, beets, potato skins, rice, sugarcane, wheat, and even yard clippings. However, using edible crops for fuel may not be a wise solution, so scientists are exploring other options.

Propelled by Peanuts

➡ **BIOFUELS** aren't new. When Dr. Rudolf Christian Karl Diesel invented his diesel engine in the 1890s, it first ran on peanut oil. When Henry Ford invented the Model T in 1908, he planned to fuel it with ethanol made from processed plant sugars.

➡ Inventors stopped exploring biofuels when discoveries of huge petroleum deposits made **GASOLINE** and **DIESEL OIL** cheap to buy.

▶ Biofuels became popular again in the early 1990s, when **ETHANOL** from corn began to be added to gasoline to help reduce carbon dioxide emissions. Biofuels currently provide about 3 percent of the energy used in the United States.

Grass by the Gallon

Switchgrass is grown at the University of Alabama's test plot near Auburn, Alabama.

▶ **"GRASSOLINE"** is the nickname for fuel developed from switchgrass, which grows in the United States, Canada, Central and South America, and parts of Africa. It is fast-growing and hardy, needs little fertilizer, and contains lots of cellulose, an important ingredient in ethanol.

SLIME TIME

▶ **ALGAE,** such as in the green film you see on a fish tank, is among the world's fastest-growing plants and is a useful biofuel. Algae grows in dirty water, even sewage, using up carbon dioxide as it spreads. The energy stored inside algae cells can be converted into transportation fuel, and the proteins that the algae produce can be used to make animal feed.

CONTINUED

s, all for a greener tomorrow.

Dartmouth's two Big Green Buses have logged more than 45,000 miles on diesel engines converted to run on waste vegetable oil.

FUN ON THE "FRYBRID"

Every summer since 2005, students from Dartmouth College have traveled across the United States aboard a **BIG GREEN BUS** with a diesel engine that has been converted to run on waste vegetable oil, or WVO. (The bus's fuel system has a filter to catch fries and other food particles that may still be floating in the WVO.) It always refuels at restaurants and "could smell like fries, burgers, or Mexican or Chinese food," according to one of the students.

As more people drive WVO-fueled vehicles, WVO has become more popular and some restaurants have begun to sell it.

Fat Is Where It's At

Researchers at the University of Arkansas combine chicken fat with tall oil fatty acid (a by-product of wood pulp) to produce fuel by subjecting the mixture to high temperature and pressure.

STEP ON THE . . . AIR

A company called Zero Pollution Motors (ZPM) will soon be introducing in North America a car called the **"FlowAIR."** Powered by a compressed air engine, it runs on air and emits only air.

An artist's rendering of the compressed air vehicle developed by MDI in France. It will be manufactured in the United States by Zero Pollution Motors in 2010.

The Power of Poop

➡ The Toronto Zoo estimates that its 5,000 animals produce enough MANURE to power a biogas-to-electricity plant, which would supply all of the zoo's needs as well as produce surplus electricity that could be sold to the city.

➡ A company called Norcal Waste in San Francisco collects DOG WASTE from containers in city parks. A special process converts this poop into methane gas, which can be used to power anything that normally runs on natural gas.

GET GOING!
What's your idea for the best new energy source? Share it at Almanac4kids.com /tellus.

HOLD YOUR NOSE!

Q What's green and purple and smelly all over?

A SKUNK CABBAGE!

These bold plants sink their roots into wet, woodland areas or other mushy places, such as marshes and bogs. Eastern skunk cabbage is found from Nova Scotia and southern Quebec south to Tennessee. Western skunk cabbage thrives from Cook Inlet, Alaska, all the way down to central California.

Some skunk cabbage plants live for more than 100 years. The older the plant is, the more firmly it sits in the wet ground. This is because it has contractile roots that grow downward and then contract, or shrink, pulling the plant stem deeper.

🍃 The SKUNK CABBAGE FLOWER appears before the leaves, usually in February or early March. As the flower comes out of the ground, it produces enough heat to melt ice and snow and provide a toasty shelter for insects. The area inside the flower can be up to 50 degrees warmer than the outside air.

🍃 The EASTERN SKUNK CABBAGE FLOWER has a tall, curved leaf (called a **spathe**) that looks like a pointed hood and is mottled purple and green—the color of rotting meat.

🍃 The Eastern variety's spathe surrounds a bumpy, egg-shape spike (or **spadix**) that is covered with tiny, petal-less flowers that smell like rotting meat—at least to certain flies and other insects. The spadix is yellow at first but changes to dark red or black while seeds ripen. (The WESTERN VERSION has a bright-yellow spathe and a tall, green spadix.)

continued

In spring, the bright-green SKUNK CABBAGE LEAVES unfurl and quickly expand to as much as 4 feet long. In midsummer, the leaves dissolve into a slimy, black mess and disappear.

Crushed skunk cabbage leaves smell like skunk spray mixed with onions. Black bears, turkeys, and a few other animals love skunk cabbages. They eat the leaves and other parts of the plant. (Skunk cabbage is not food for humans. Don't eat any part of it. Your mouth and throat would swell and burn, and you could get very sick.)

BIG STINKERS

Some of the largest flowers in the world attract pollinators in the same way that skunk cabbage does—by smelling like ROTTING MEAT.

CORPSE FLOWER grows in Indonesia and comes from the same family as skunk cabbage. It contains many tiny flowers growing together. The entire blossom grows up to 10 feet tall, and the plant itself can weigh more than 170 pounds.

STINKING CORPSE LILY is the world's largest single flower. It grows to about 3 feet wide and weighs as much as 24 pounds. It is also native to Indonesia.

YOU ARE MY Sunshine

Grow these dazzling beauties and watch heads turn.

Like kids, sunflowers come in many sizes. The common sunflower can grow to be 6 feet tall or higher. Some sunflower varieties, such as 'Teddy Bear' and 'Junior', stop growing at 3 feet, and dwarf sunflowers, like 'Sunny Smile' and 'Choco Sun', reach no higher than your knee.

Sunflowers with big brown centers and bright-yellow petals are a familiar sight. Becoming popular because they are different are new varieties with petals of orange, creamy white, pink, dark red, gold, copper, or bronze.

In their bud stage, sunflowers turn their heads to follow the Sun during the day. When they are in bloom, they face east. Why they do this is a mystery. Some people think that the plants may be protecting their seeds from the Sun's mid- and late-day heat.

DID YOU KNOW?

❀ Native Americans used sunflowers as early as 3000 B.C. They ate sunflower seeds whole or pounded them into meal for cakes and breads. They also squeezed oil out of the seeds and used it for cooking and as a body lotion.

❀ In Kansas, the "Sunflower State," sunflowers are so abundant that they are considered weeds.

❀ The tallest sunflower on record was 25 feet 5.4 inches tall. It was grown in the Netherlands.

❀ The largest sunflower head ever measured was 32.3 inches across at its widest point. It was grown in British Columbia.

CONTINUED

Grow a Sunflower Tower

If you have space in your yard (and your parents allow it), grow a sunflower tower that you can go inside.

Find a spot with lots of sunshine.

You will need a packet or two of sunflower seeds that will grow at least 6 feet tall. Read the back of the packet to see what size you have.

❀ At sunset, cut a sunflower while making a wish.
The wish will come true the next day. *–folklore*

Using sticks and string, mark off an area in your garden where you want your sunflower tower to be or borrow a garden hose and lay it on the perimeter of your tower. Make the tower circular, square, rectangular, even triangular, but make sure that it is at least 8 feet across. Measure it with a yardstick, tape, or ruler.

With a shovel, dig along the marked area. Dig down about a foot to loosen the soil. Be sure to leave an undug portion on one side for a doorway that's wide enough to walk through.

Plant the sunflower seeds 6 inches apart and an inch deep. For thick walls, plant two rows of seeds, leaving about 1 foot between rows. Be creative: Plant 3-foot sunflowers for the next outside row. If you have space, add another outside row of a shorter, knee-high variety.

Water the seeds well every day. They should start to sprout in a week, if the weather is warm. Sunflowers usually reach their full height in about 10 weeks.

If you want your sunflower tower to have a roof, plant morning glory seeds among the sunflower seeds. As the plants grow, the morning glories will climb the sunflower stalks. When the sunflowers start to bud, tie string or twine to the sunflower stems and across the top. The morning glories will follow the string, putting a top on your tower.

BE A BIRD BUDDY

After your sunflowers have grown to maturity and the seeds have dried, cut off the flower heads and put them where birds can easily eat the seeds.

A GOLDFINCH

NATURE'S SNACK PACK

❀ If you don't grow your own sunflowers and harvest the seeds, you can buy some to eat. The seeds have an outer shell, or hull. You crack it with your teeth and discard the hull. Inside is the kernel, or meat. Kernels are a healthy snack that can be roasted in the oven (ask an adult for help) or eaten raw.

IN THE GARDEN

GROW PLANTS

A terrarium is a miniature ecosystem with soil and plants. It creates its own atmosphere and needs little help—only sunlight. Moisture that condenses on the glass runs down the inside to moisten the soil. A covered container protects the plants from insects, diseases, and dry indoor air.

UNDER GLASS

YOU WILL NEED:

- a clear glass container, such as a small aquarium, a big fishbowl, or a big mayonnaise jar
- pebbles or small aquarium stones
- activated charcoal (available at most pet stores)
- potting soil
- peat moss
- plants (the number will depend on their size and the size of your container)
- a few rocks and twigs
- glass or clear plastic, if a container lid is not available

1 Clean the container, using warm, soapy water. Rinse well and dry.

2 Cover the bottom of the container with a 1-inch layer of pebbles or aquarium stones. Add small chunks of charcoal.

3 In a separate bucket, mix moist potting soil and peat moss. Add 2 inches of this to the terrarium and press it down. Mold a portion of the soil into hills and valleys to add interest (depending on the size of your container).

POTTING SOIL MIXTURE

CHARCOAL
PEBBLES

■ Ancient Greeks were the first to grow plants in transparent containers.

■ Dr. Nathan Ward of London, England, accidentally invented the terrarium in the early 1800s. He placed a cocoon in a covered jar in order to watch the emergence of a sphinx moth. In time, several plants, including a fern (which he had been unsuccessful in growing outside), sprang up from the soil in the jar. Nathan set about constructing several fern containers. These glass gardens were later called Wardian cases and became very popular.

4 Dig small holes in the soil. Set plants in the holes and cover the roots with soil. Leave room to grow.

5 Moderately water the plants.

6 Add a few rocks and small twigs for a natural-looking setting.

7 Cover the top of the terrarium.

Keep your terrarium out of direct sunlight to avoid overheating. If the sides fog up from excess humidity, leave the top open a bit so that some of the moisture can evaporate.

■ New England housewives were the first to use terrariums in North America. They grew partridgeberry in hand-blown, glass bowls.

Plant Picks

Take a walk in the woods to gather moss and plants (avoid endangered species and be sure not to select specimens with insects, parasites, or signs of disease) or try small houseplants such as these, available at nurseries:

- **begonia**
- **miniature fern**
- **small peperomia**
- **African violet**
- **ivy**

The BEET GOES ON

In ancient times, when beets were discovered to be edible, people loved them mainly for their leaves, or greens, perhaps because it was the only part they could see. Beet greens are nutritious and delicious, but to many people the beetroot is the best.

Beets are easy to grow. The most popular beet is red, but they can also be yellow, white, and red-and-white-striped. The striped variety is called 'Chioggia'. Beets grow in many sizes, from as small as a golf ball to as big as a baseball. Small beets are called baby beets and sometimes can be eaten in one bite!

Beets like full sun and sandy soil. Sow beet seeds in the spring, as soon as the soil becomes crumbly and the daytime temperature reaches 60°F. Set the seeds ½-inch deep in the soil, about 2 inches apart. Water lightly with a spray nozzle on a hose or watering can (a strong stream of water could push the seeds out of the ground).

When the plants are 2 inches tall, thin them by picking out every other one. (If you have space, try replanting these.) Ask an adult to help you fertilize your beet plants. Keep the soil around your beets free of weeds by pulling the weeds out gently. Water the plants regularly. With proper care, the beets will be ready to pick in 55 to 70 days. Check your seed packet for the specific growing time.

Leaf It Alone

Trim off the stems, rinse, and chop or tear up the leaves. Steam the leaves or eat them raw in salads.

BEETS

(continued)

Have a Bake-Off

Ask an adult for help with this. Preheat the oven to 400°F. Rinse three or four beets under the faucet, then wipe them dry with a paper towel. Cut off the root tail and leaves. Place the beets in a baking dish. Add water to reach about ½-inch up the sides of the dish. Cover the beets loosely with aluminum foil. Bake for 1 hour, or until the beets feel tender when pierced with a fork. Carefully remove the dish from the oven, uncover, and set aside. When the beets are cool enough to handle, peel off the skin and eat. Beets taste great by themselves, but experiment by adding herbs and spices like dill, chives, garlic, or parsley.

Beetroots can also be boiled, sautéed, steamed, or pickled.

SNACK ATTACK. To make beet chips, go to Almanac4kids.com/beets.

DID YOU KNOW?

In colonial times, beet dye was used to add color to icing for cakes and to make pink pancakes.

● In 1975, when the *Apollo 18* spacecraft and the Soviet Union's *Soyuz 19* linked up in space, the cosmonauts served the astronauts beet soup, called borscht, squeezed from tubes.

In Australia, pickled beets—not cucumber pickles—are served on hamburgers.

● Dye from pulverized beets is used to turn lemonade pink, to tint the tomato sauce on frozen pizzas red, and to make ink used by butchers to label meat.

● Of all the vegetables dehydrated for use during World War II (1939–45), beets dried out the best.

Name That Vegetable

Match the clues with the correct vegetables.

1. My inside can be up to 20 degrees Fahrenheit cooler than my outside. I am 95 percent water.

2. I am mostly used for decoration, not to eat, but some people make me into a pie.

3. I can be found in a gumbo, and I'm mostly grown in the southern states.

4. I am usually purple; some people call me aubergine.

5. Ethanol and flour are made from me. I can be found in grits and hominy.

6. Garlic and leeks are my cousins.

7. If I'm not picked, I will grow into a large, fernlike plant.

8. I am a dried and smoked hot pepper.

9. I'm very starchy, I grow in the dark, and I have eyes that do not see.

10. Hippocrates used my leaves as bandages to help in healing wounds around 400 B.C. Be careful, or I will stain everything I touch.

a. **asparagus**
b. **beet**
c. **chipotle**
d. **corn**
e. **cucumber**
f. **eggplant**
g. **okra**
h. **onion**
i. **potato**
j. **pumpkin**

Answers: 1. e; 2. j; 3. g; 4. f; 5. d; 6. h; 7. a; 8. c; 9. i; 10. b

SCRUBBABLE

LOO

Loofah, or luffa, is a gourd that becomes a sponge. It is easy and fun to grow.

Loofah seeds need help getting started. Scratch, or SCARIFY, the outside of each seed with sandpaper or a nail file (get help, if necessary) and soak them in water for 1 to 2 days.

The plants need about 4 months to grow. If you live in a warm climate, sow seeds in the ground in spring. If you live in a cold climate, start the seeds indoors in peat pots in late March or early April.

- Fill peat pots about two-thirds full of soil.
- Put one seed in each pot and cover with ¾-inch of soil.
- Add water to dampen.
- Place the pots in a sunny, warm place.

Water regularly to keep the soil moist. The seeds will sprout in 2 to 3 weeks. When the seedlings' second pair of leaves appears, put the plants outside in a semi-shady spot for a couple of hours. This

WHAT'S A PEAT POT?

Peat pots are made of peat moss, a natural material that breaks up in the soil. The pot, with the plant and growing soil in it, are set into the ground. The plant's roots will grow through the pot, and it will eventually disintegrate.

LOVABLE

FAH

hardens them off, or gets them used to being outdoors. Do this for 6 to 8 days, increasing the time and sunlight each day.

Loofah needs space, and something to climb, like a strong trellis or fence. Be prepared: The vines can grow to 20 feet tall or higher, and the fruit will rot if it touches the ground.

When you plant, dig a hole about a foot deep and fill it with compost. Place the peat pot in the center with its top just below the surface. Fill in with compost and pat it down gently. Or, place a presoaked seed on the compost and cover it with ¾-inch of soil.

Water now and often as the plants grow.

CONTINUED • • • • • • • • • • • • • • • • ➤

Watch for large yellow flowers to appear. Many of these will develop tiny green fruits that will become gourds. To get sponges, leave the fruit on the vine as long as possible. Pick the gourds when they are 12 to 18 inches long, with brown and leathery skin and seeds that rattle inside if the gourd is shaken. (If a frost is coming, pick the gourds immediately.)

Store the gourds in a warm, dry place. When the skin becomes papery, peel it off. Cut off the blossom end and shake out the seeds. Rinse the loofah thoroughly in water. Dry the sponge outside, if possible, on a warm, sunny day.

Now, go wash up!

Make Sn'c

Carefully cut a dry loofah sponge into ¼- to ½-inch-wide slices. Paint the slices white or use them as is. Draw a ribbon or string

in becomes papery, peel it off.

Beyond the Bath

In addition to serving as packing material, light but tough loofah fiber has been used in . . .

- pot scrubbers
- baskets, carpets, and doormats
- industrial insulation and filters
- sound and shock absorbers in military helmets
- pillows and mattresses
- slipper soles

INCREDIBLE:
IT'S EDIBLE, TOO!

When loofah fruit is 3 to 4 inches long, it can be cooked like summer squash and eaten.

h Flakes

through an opening in the edge of the sponge and tie it off. Hang the sn'oofah flake in a window or on a Christmas tree.

Scare TACTICS

Throughout history, farmers have been trying to protect their crops from birds, rodents, wolves, coyotes, and even evil spirits.

Farmers in ancient Egypt jumped out from behind net-covered wooden frames to shoo away birds.

In ancient Japan, growers protected their rice crops with scarecrows made from rotting meat, old rags, and fish bones hung on poles. When set on fire, the garbage produced stench that drove off animals. Later, Japanese farmers used scarecrows that wore coats and hats made from reeds.

In medieval Germany, farmers populated their fields with wooden witches to drive off the evil spirit of winter and encourage the early arrival of spring. Meanwhile, farmers in Italy put animal skulls on poles to scare away birds and disease. In some parts of Europe, boys would patrol farmers' fields, banging wooden blocks, or "clappers," to frighten

Ahboosh! Ahboosh!

crows—until the Great Plague of 1348, when a horrible disease transmitted by fleas caused the deaths of many children. Farmers then had to resort to making bird scarers with gourd or turnip heads and straw bodies.

In the 1800s, German farmers in Pennsylvania used old clothes to make a *bootzaman,* or bogeyman, and *bootzafrau,* his wife.

In the late 19th century, Native American Zuni children made figures with rags, dog or coyote skins, and bones hanging on yucca fiber ropes. The racket made by bones dangling in the breeze scared off many birds.

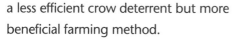

At about the same time, some American farmers stopped using scarecrows and instead offered a bounty for dead crows. Thousands of birds were killed before the farmers realized that they needed crows to devour the corn borers and other insects that ate their crops. Soon they removed the bounty and returned to making scarecrows, a less efficient crow deterrent but more beneficial farming method.

Today, commercial farmers scare away crows with noisemakers, spinning whirligigs, flashing lights, hawk silhouettes, or plastic ribbons that wave in the wind and shimmer in the sunlight. It's mostly small farmers, home gardeners, and kids who make and display straw-stuffed figures in overalls, flannel shirts, and floppy hats.

SHARE A SCARE!

Make a scarecrow or find one in your neighborhood, take a picture of it, and send it to Almanac4kids.com/scarecrow, with a brief story about how you made it or why you like it.

All About THE ALL-AMER

Turkeys **originated over 10 million years ago** in North America. Wild turkeys live in the woods and spend nights in trees. Domesticated turkeys live on farms and are twice as big as wild birds, making them too heavy to fly.

Traditionally, turkeys have been raised outdoors, on farms. "Free-range" turkeys are allowed to strut about in the farmyard. "Heritage" turkeys are old-fashioned breeds.

Turkeys have great hearing and pretty good vision. They can hear sounds a mile away and see slight movement in daylight—but not at night.

ON THE FARM

Wild turkeys can run at up to 30 miles per hour (but not for far) and fly at up to 55 miles per hour (but not for long).

By the 1930s, almost all of the wild turkeys in the United States had been hunted. Today, thanks to conservation programs, there are plenty of wild turkeys—and they are invading some cities. These almost-4-foot-tall birds have been spotted on sidewalks near Boston, prompting people to call the police!

BIRDS OF A FEATHER

- **TOM:** a male turkey or gobbler

- **HEN:** a female turkey

- **JAKE:** a young male

- **POULT:** a baby turkey

CONTINUED

Farmers have to protect their birds from predators, such as coyotes and owls, and they also have to pay attention to weather conditions that could harm their flocks.

As Americans began eating more turkey all year-round (not just at Thanksgiving), many turkey breeders began raising the birds in places that look more like factories than farms.

SPEAKING OF EATING

A turkey's breast muscles are for flying, but they are seldom used. There are few blood vessels there, and little oxygen is delivered to them—which is why breast meat is white.

Turkeys run around a lot, so their leg and thigh muscles have many oxygen-carrying blood vessels—which is why leg and thigh meat is dark.

Nobody is sure if the pilgrims ate turkey at their first thanksgiving feast in 1621. One account doesn't mention turkey; another does, but it was written 20 years later. It wasn't until after 1863, the year when President Abraham Lincoln made Thanksgiving Day a national holiday, that turkeys began to land on dinner platters across the country.

Every November since 1947, a "National Thanksgiving Turkey" has been presented to the U.S. president. Harry Truman got that first one. During an official ceremony in the Rose Garden, the president "pardons" the turkey, meaning that its life is spared and it does not get eaten. In November, go to www.whitehouse.gov and vote to help name the National Turkey.

BIRD WORDS

A turkey will stand in the rain and stare straight up at the rain-drops until it drowns.

FALSE!

Turkeys do go out in the rain. Young ones that do and are not yet covered in their true feathers will sometimes catch a cold and later die from exposure.

The **SNOOD** is a flap of skin above a turkey's beak.

The **DEWLAP** connects the head to the neck, under the beak.

CARUNCLES are bright-pink growths on a turkey's throat.

Poults pile up in a corner to sleep and sometimes smother each other.

TRUE!

That's why farmers round out the corners in coops, provide fresh air, and keep the room temperature comfortable.

No one knows for sure what the caruncles or snood are for. These body parts turn red, white, and blue when a male turkey is upset or courting.

CONTINUED

Think You've Heard Everything?

A Florida man named Joe Hutto raised wild turkeys and taught himself to communicate with them. He spent almost every moment with his flock and began to feel like a turkey. "I spoke to them, and they, in turn, talked to me, too," he said. Joe learned that turkeys have a vocabulary of at least 50 different signals. Here is a sampling:

"Gobble, gobble" is made by a tom and means "Hey, hens, check me out!" It also serves as a warning to other toms to stay away.

A **cluck** means "Hey, you!" It gets another turkey's attention.

Cackling means "Look out, below!" and is often done by excited hens as they fly down from their roosts.

A **yelp** is turkey talk for "Good morning!" Three or four yelps are normal.

Purring means that a turkey is content.

Listen to turkey talk at
Almanac4kids.com/turkey.

TURKEY

● There are several theories about how turkeys got their name. One story claims that Christopher Columbus heard some birds say, "tuka, tuka," and his interpreter came up with the name *tukki*, which means "big bird" in Hebrew.

Gobble, gobble!

QUIRKY TURKEY

NUGGETS

- Turkeys perched on trees and refusing to descend indicates snow. *—folklore*

- A dance called the Turkey Trot became popular in the early 1900s. As music played, a dancer made a series of quick hopping steps like a turkey.

- The original TV dinner, introduced in 1952, contained turkey.

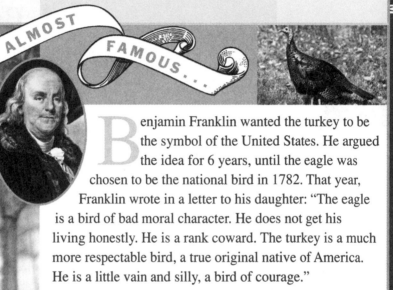

ALMOST FAMOUS...

Benjamin Franklin wanted the turkey to be the symbol of the United States. He argued the idea for 6 years, until the eagle was chosen to be the national bird in 1782. That year, Franklin wrote in a letter to his daughter: "The eagle is a bird of bad moral character. He does not get his living honestly. He is a rank coward. The turkey is a much more respectable bird, a true original native of America. He is a little vain and silly, a bird of courage."

FOWL PLAY

How do you *score* a "turkey"? Bowl three strikes in a row. In the early 1900s, during the Thanksgiving and Christmas holidays, people who bowled three strikes in a row were often rewarded with a live turkey.

➡ A turkey vulture only looks like a turkey. It is a high-flying buzzard with a bald, red head and a great sense of smell. Its primary method of defending against attack is vomiting!

The BUZZ on

Bee-ginnings

The Latin word for "bee" is *APIS*.

Beekeeping is called APICULTURE.

A beekeeper is an APIARIST.

A collection of beehives is an APIARY.

ithout honeybees, many farmers and gardeners would not have a harvest. Bees transfer pollen from flower to flower, or pollinate, which helps fruits and vegetables to form.

Honeybees are found in nature, but they are also kept and nurtured by beekeepers. Some beekeepers raise bees for their honey and other products. Some breed honeybees for sale. Others drive truckloads of hives across the country to rent their bees to farmers as crops such as almonds and apples come into flower.

A colony is a community of honeybees. In summer, a colony contains one queen, a few thousand drones (males), and tens of thousands of worker bees (females). In winter, populations are much smaller and usually lack drones. The queen's sole purpose is to lay eggs. The drones' only job is to mate with the queen. Worker bees work: They provide the food; build, repair, and clean the hive; guard against intruders; and raise the young.

Worker   Drone   Queen

A Few Things About Stings

- A worker bee can sting once. It dies soon after.

- A drone has no stinger.

- A queen honeybee can sting repeatedly.

BEES

continued

Bees will not swarm before

Beekeepers house bees in hives, consisting of one or more stackable boxes, or hive bodies. Inside each hive body hang nine or ten frames with a sheet of beeswax in the center. Worker bees build honeycomb on the beeswax and store food in many of its cells. The queen lays her eggs in separate honeycomb cells. Bees enter the hive through an opening in the bottom.

Gloves and long sleeves protect a beekeeper as he checks the frames in the hive.

When a hive becomes overcrowded, bees swarm. The old queen, a few drones, and thousands of worker bees — about half of the colony — leave the hive and settle on a tree branch or other object until bee scouts can find a suitable nesting site, such as a tree cavity.

In swarms and alone, honeybees are normally gentle. They usually do not attack people unless they are threatened. Strong odors and dark or fuzzy clothing that resembles an animal can be threatening. If a beekeeper thinks that his hive bees feel threatened, he will use a smoker, which burns wood, burlap, straw, cotton waste, pine needles, or other fuel to create a

ear storm. *–proverb*

cloud that disperses the bees, dulls their senses, and makes them hungry for a short while. (Some bees eat so much honey when they are smoked that it's difficult for them to sting.)

To be safe, beekeepers wear special, light-color clothing when handling a hive. A hat and veil protect the head and neck, and gloves or gauntlets protect the hands and lower arms. Many cover their ankles and close their pant legs with a string or have elastic-band cuffs so that bees don't climb up their legs. Angry bees often attack ankles first because they are closest to the hive's entrance.

Using a smoker helps to calm the bees when they become agitated.

OH, HONEY!

A healthy beehive can produce 45 to 100 pounds of honey per year—often more than the bees need to survive. Keepers harvest the excess by removing the frames, scraping off the beeswax caps on the honeycomb cells, and then spinning the frames in an extractor (this removes the honey from the comb). The honey is strained to remove any bits of wax or debris and then bottled. The color and flavor of the honey is influenced by the flowers that the honeybees visit. There are more than 300 kinds of honey in the United States, including these two: pale, mild-tasting, alfalfa honey and dark, malty, buckwheat honey.

continued

BEE WARY

- Bears love honey, and they also love to eat honeybees. Other honeybee predators include skunks, raccoons, opossums, birds, and spiders.

A parasitic *Varroa* mite on the back of a European honeybee.

- Mites can cripple or kill honeybees.
- Pesticides, pollution, and shrinking natural habitat threaten bees.

Why do bees have sticky hair?

Because they have honeycombs.

BEE-LIEVE IT OR NOT...

In the 1920s, to say "it's the bee's knees" meant that something was really terrific.

On June 14, 2004, a tractor-trailer overturned on a highway in Bear Trap Canyon, Montana, spilling its load of hundreds of beehives and unleashing some 9 million angry honeybees.

In 1998, Mark Biancaniello from California, *below,* set a world record as the person covered with the most bees: 87½ pounds of them (estimated to be 350,000 bees). He was aided by bee experts, who knew how to attract the bees and safely handle them.

A life-size cow and calf made entirely of butter, on display at the Ohio State Fair in August 2007

BUTTER FINGERS!

The next time your parents tell you not to play with your food, ask them if they've ever heard of BUTTER SCULPTORS.

The first butter sculptures in North America were probably made by frontier and farm women. They churned their own butter and set it in molds to give it shape and a decorative pattern.

Serious butter sculpting in America began at the 1876 Centennial Exhibition in Philadelphia, when Caroline Shawk Brooks displayed a woman's face rendered in butter. She called her portrait *Dreaming Iolanthe*. Since this was before the invention of refrigeration, Caroline kept the butter cool by placing a bucket of ice below it.

CONTINUED

The cow is of the bovine il‹

Soon, managers of large dairies began using butter sculptures to advertise their companies, particularly at state fairs. As improvements in electrical refrigeration made it easier to keep the butter cool, sculptures of all shapes and sizes became state fair favorites.

For the 1901 Pan-American Exposition in Buffalo, New York, John K. Daniels and his brother worked for 6 weeks and used 1,000 pounds of butter to sculpt an 11-foot-long, 5-foot 4-inch–high model of Minnesota's then-new capitol.

At an exposition in St. Louis in 1904, the butter sculptures included a life-size explorer and two guides in a canoe, two portraits of Teddy Roosevelt, and several cows.

The Butter Cow Lady

Norma "Duffy" Lyon wanted to be a veterinarian, but this wasn't an easy career path for a woman in the 1940s. Instead, she helped her husband run the family farm. She saw her first butter cow at an Iowa State Fair in the late 1950s. She began helping the sculptor, and in 1960 she took over completely. Duffy continued to butter sculpt until her retirement in 2006.

Watch the "Butter Cow Lady" make a cow at www.thebuttercowlady.com.

Butter Basics

Butter sculpting is best done when temperatures are about 38° to 40°F. Today, most artists work in a refrigerated room.

Large butter sculptures are usually hollow. The artist begins with a metal or wooden frame on which mesh or another material is applied to give the form shape. The butter is then applied in layers and sculpted. The process may take days or weeks, depending on the sculpture.

One end is moo, the other, milk. *–Ogden Nash, American poet (1902–71)*

To make one life-size cow, a sculptor needs about 600 pounds of butter (that's enough for almost 20,000 slices of toast). Sculptors don't buy butter in sticks. Dairies or dairy associations often provide it in bulk.

Butter sculptures can last for months if they are refrigerated. Sometimes the butter is reused for other sculptures for as long as 10 years.

Fair-goers watch as slabs of butter are transformed into works of art at the 2007 Royal Agricultural Winter Fair in Toronto.

The Butter Princess

EACH YEAR AT THE MINNESOTA STATE FAIR, a young woman is crowned as the state dairy princess. On the first day of the fair, the new princess enters a refrigerated booth where, for 6 to 8 hours, an artist sculpts her head and shoulders out of a 90-pound block of butter made especially for the fair. The sculpture goes on display and the princess gets to take it home after the fair.

Some princess sculptures are put on display at restaurants or other public places. One princess's grandmother used the butter to make Christmas cookies. Another sculpture was stored in a barn for the winter. When a neighbor saw the sculpture, he thought that it was a person and called the police!

· · · · · · · · · · · · · **NAME-DROPPING** · · · · · · · · · · · ·

In sports, a "butterfingers" is someone who does not hold on to a ball that ought to be caught or handled. The phrase is commonly used to describe someone who drops things.

GOT GE

THE FOOTBALL HELMET

During the 1880s, football players thought that long hair would help to protect them from head injuries by cushioning the impact when they hit the ground or each other. In 1893, Joseph M. Reeves, a player on the U.S. Naval Academy team who had taken numerous head poundings, paid a horse harness maker to create a leather cap for him to use in an upcoming game against the U.S. Military Academy. Navy won the game, in which Joseph became the first football player ever to wear headgear.

Later, caps with straps, earflaps, and nose protectors were tried.

In 1939, Gerry E. Morgan and the John T. Riddell Company in Chicago patented the first football helmet. It was plastic and had a strap that enabled the player to tighten it onto his head. Riddell's helmet softened impact better than leather caps, provided better ventilation, and lasted longer. It was also lighter and wouldn't rot or mildew like leather.

Over time, chin straps were added and less-brittle plastic was used. Today, Riddell's design, made with state-of-the-art materials, continues to be one of the most popular.

FILL 'ER UP

In the 1970s, some football players used "micro-fit" helmets that had valves on the outside and a vinyl sac inside. Air or water was blown into the sac, making a form-fitting cushion around the player's head. Because the water could turn to ice in cold weather, sometimes antifreeze was used instead.

THE CATCHER'S MITT

Baseball was originally a bare-handed game. Wearing gloves was a sign of weakness; players were expected to endure any pain. In 1870, Cincinnati Red Stockings catcher Doug Allison decided that his aching hands needed some help. For a game between the Stockings and the Washington Nationals, he put on half-fingered, buckskin mittens. This was the first time that a major league baseball player officially used a glove in a game.

CONTINUED

Kansas City Blues catcher Joe Gunson is believed to have created the first catcher's "mitt" when, in 1888, he stitched together the fingers of his left-hand glove. Inspired to make a good idea better, Joe made a padded glove, using the wire handle from a pot of paint, flannel scraps, and sheepskin, which he then covered with buckskin.

A couple of years later, ex-catcher Harry Decker stitched a pillowlike pad to a glove and, with Paul Buckley, received a patent for the idea.

Today, most catchers use mitts with a hinge that closes the glove around the ball on impact.

FAST FACTS

Professional pitchers can throw baseballs at more than 90 miles per hour. On August 20, 1974, pitcher Nolan Ryan, then of the California Angels, threw a 100.9-mph fastball, setting a world record. Imagine catching that with your bare hands—ouch!

THE SOCCER BALL

Soccer players in the 13th century used balls made from inflated pig bladders, but because these vary in size and shape (no two are alike), the way the balls bounced and rolled was unpredictable.

In 1855, Charles Goodyear designed a soccer ball made of vulcanized rubber panels glued together at the seams. With an animal bladder inside, the new rubber ball held its shape better than any pig bladder.

Seven years later, H. J. Lindon created one of the first inflatable rubber bladders. (People were reportedly getting sick from blowing up animal bladders.) These could be placed inside an outer covering, such as leather.

During the 20th century, leather panels were sewn together inside out, leaving a small opening so that the leather could be turned right side out. A rubber bladder was inserted and inflated, and the hole was then stitched shut. However, heading such a ball on its stitches could sometimes hurt, and, if it rained and the leather got wet, the ball could become heavy (also hard on the head). Later improvements made the ball waterproof, more durable (without stitches), and better able to hold its shape.

Today, soccer balls are made from new, high-tech materials and designs.

HEADS UP!

The first soccer game played with a Goodyear ball took place on the Boston Common on November 7, 1863, between a team from the Boston Latin and Boston English Schools and students from Dixwell Latin School. Today, that ball resides in the National Soccer Hall of Fame in Oneonta, New York.

Baseball's "CYCLONE"

Denton True Young was born on a farm in 1867 in Tuscarawas County, Ohio. Farm chores made Dent big and strong: He grew to be 6 feet 2 inches tall and 210 pounds. When work was done, he loved to play baseball. He wasn't a particularly good hitter, but, oh, how he could pitch!

In 1890, Dent began playing for a minor league team in Canton, Ohio. Heads turned when he threw his fastball, even though some would elude the catcher and crash against the fence. One sportswriter said, "It looks like a cyclone hit it!" This is how Dent got his nickname, "Cyclone," which was soon shortened to "Cy."

The Canton team didn't do well, but Cy did. By August, he had been invited to play for the Cleveland Spiders, a major league team at that time. During his first game, on August 6 against the Chicago White Stockings, the opposing manager and first baseman, Adrian "Cap" Anson, jeered and laughed—until he saw Cy in action. Then he tried to buy out Cy's contract but couldn't. Cy's team wanted to keep him.

Cy played baseball for the next 21 seasons. In 1903, he helped the Boston Americans (now the Red Sox) to win the World Series. His career accomplishments remain legendary:

- ⚾ **511 victories, almost 100 more than any other pitcher**
- ⚾ **7,356 innings pitched (the most)**

- 816 games started (the most)
- 751 complete games pitched (the most)

Cy threw three no-hitters, including the first perfect game in baseball's modern era on May 5, 1904, against the Philadelphia Athletics. He had been so focused on finishing the game that he didn't realize what he had accomplished. His excited Boston teammates mobbed him and presented him with the game ball.

When he retired to his Ohio farm in 1911, Cy had a sore arm, but he preferred to blame his increased waistline for not being able to play baseball as well as he once did. He was inducted into the National Baseball Hall of Fame in 1937 and died at age 88 in 1955.

PERFECT PITCH ➡ To throw a "perfect" game, a pitcher must not allow any batters to reach base, whether by hits, walks, fielder's errors, or being hit by a pitch. This has happened only 17 times in major league history (as of 2008).

WHY WE Love Cy

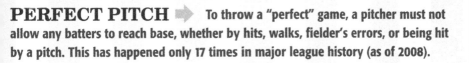

- Before 1896, Cy didn't wear a baseball glove (many players didn't at the time).

- Cy stayed in shape during the off-season by chopping wood and doing heavy chores on his farm.

- Although he had only a sixth-grade education, Cy loved to have his wife read aloud the writings of Charles Dickens, William Makepeace Thackeray, and Mark Twain.

- As the starting pitcher for Boston in 1903, Cy threw the first pitch in the very first World Series game.

The AWARD and the WINNERS

The first Cy Young Award was given to Brooklyn Dodgers pitcher Don Newcombe in 1956. For the next 10 years, it was given to the top major league pitcher. Starting in 1967, one award was given to an American League pitcher and another to a National League pitcher. Winners have included Whitey Ford, Sandy Koufax, Roger Clemens, Randy Johnson, Pedro Martínez, and CC Sabathia. Members of the Baseball Writers Association of America decide the winners.

HOOKED ON THE OUTDOORS

How a young girl went fishing and landed fame

Cornelia Thurza Crosby was born in the tiny town of Phillips, Maine, on November 10, 1854. When she was nearly 2 years old, her father died of tuberculosis, a lung disease also known as TB. When she was 13, her brother died of the same disease. Cornelia had TB too, so in an attempt to improve her health, doctors told her to spend as much time as possible outdoors. This was easy because mountains, rivers, and streams surrounded her hometown, and it was lucky because being outside led her to catch her first fish.

Despite the hardships, Cornelia had many advantages over other girls. She attended a private school in Augusta, Maine, for 2 years, paying the tuition with an inheritance of $600. Her education later helped her to get jobs,

Cornelia "Fly Rod" Crosby

including positions as a bank clerk, telegraph operator, and publicist for the Maine Central Railroad.

Main Street, Phillips, Maine —Cornelia's hometown

As an adult, Cornelia was a Victorian lady who held tea parties, taught Sunday school, and collected china as well as fishing tackle. She dressed in the fashion of the era— long-sleeve blouses, ankle-length dresses, and knee-high boots—even when fishing. She loved the sport. She once said, "I would rather fish any day than go to heaven." She was a skilled angler. She could catch hundreds of fish in a day, which is how she got the nickname "Fly Rod."

Cornelia's health remained a problem throughout her life. Sometimes she was sick for months at a time, but as soon as she was better, she headed to the fishing and hunting camps in the woods. She hunted bear, moose, and caribou and could hike for 40 miles and paddle a canoe. Eventually, in 1897, Cornelia became the first registered Maine Guide.

In 1878, the *Phillips Phonograph* newspaper was launched in her hometown. Cornelia was first mentioned in it for winning a prize for sewing at the Phillips Show and Fair.

continued

124

At the first Sportsmen's Exposition, thousands of visitors admired Cornelia's exhibit—a log cabin she had built herself.

Before long, she was writing a column about her outdoor adventures, titled "Fly Rod's Notebook." It became so popular that many newspapers east of the Mississippi River published it. Cornelia wrote about Maine's wilderness areas, such as the Rangeley region. The Maine Central Railroad provided passenger service to many of these places, and one day, a railroad manager suggested that they hire Cornelia to promote the state and attract tourists—so they did.

In 1895, Cornelia appeared at the first Sportsmen's Exposition at Madison Square Garden in New York City. Thousands of visitors admired her exhibit, a log cabin she had built herself. The next year, attired in a green deerskin suit with a daringly short, knee-high skirt, she demonstrated fly casting, tossing her line into a tank full

Cornelia would rather fish any day than go to heaven.

of trout and salmon that she had brought from Maine for that purpose.

Cornelia realized the need to preserve Maine's wilderness and wildlife and was an early supporter of catch-and-release fishing.

In many ways, Cornelia was ahead of her time. Women in those days were expected to cook, sew, and keep busy indoors. When she died at age 93, her obituary in the Rangeley, Maine, newspaper observed: "America has lost its most famous woman sportsman."

Here Comes Cornelia

◆ At 6 feet tall, Cornelia towered over most other Victorian ladies.

◆ She was a skilled markswoman and is said to have entered a contest with her friend, sharpshooter Annie Oakley. (No word on who won!)

◆ One day, Cornelia caught 31 trout in 30 minutes.

HAVE YOU BEEN FISHING?

Tell other kids about it—where you went, what you used, the fish (or other things) that you caught—at Almanac4kids.com/tellus.

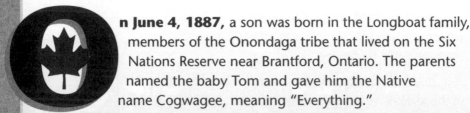

BORN TO RUN

Tom Longboat was too fast to forget.

On June 4, 1887, a son was born in the Longboat family, members of the Onondaga tribe that lived on the Six Nations Reserve near Brantford, Ontario. The parents named the baby Tom and gave him the Native name Cogwagee, meaning "Everything."

Tom loved to run. He ran to work in the fields and ran to collect the tribe's cows and herd them home. When his parents sent him away to a school for Natives, he was very unhappy, so he ran all the way home—a distance of about 12 miles.

When he was 17, Tom entered the Victoria Day 5-mile race in Caledonia. He didn't win. He came in second, and losing convinced him to train harder.

Tom's family often didn't believe his stories about how far and fast he had run. This changed on the day he beat his brother to Hamilton, about 20 miles away—even though his brother had had a head start and been driving a horse and buggy!

In 1906, Tom entered the Victoria Day race again. This time he won, with Bill Davis, another Native runner, watching.

Bill became Tom's coach and entered him in the 1906 "Around the Bay" race in Hamilton. Spectators placed bets on runners, but few people bet on Tom. Some people even laughed at him. The favorite was John Marsh from England.

Coach Davis advised Tom to follow John's pace. It was good advice. Tom did that and won the 19-mile race, nearly breaking the course record. He easily won several more races that year and started to make headlines.

CONTINUED

GENERAL VIEW OF BOSTON BY AEROPLANE.

Boston

vton

FINISH

Brookline

Framingham

Tom Longboat
running in the 1907
Boston Marathon

Boston, Mass.

Ned Hanlon, Durnan, Scholes, and Longboat of Toronto,
Canada

Tom's marathon win
was honored by a victory
parade in Toronto.

Tom ran the biggest race of his life in Boston, Massachusetts, on April 19, 1907, a cold, rainy, sleety day. Thousands turned out to watch him and the other 123 runners compete in the famous 25-mile (at that time) Boston Marathon. Reporters, some of whom had nicknamed him "The Speedy Son of the Forest," "The Indian Iron Man," and "The Running Machine," begged to interview him before and after the event.

Tom led from the start, with Charlie Petch, also from Canada, sometimes in second place. Tom was so worried that Charlie might get ahead of him that he skipped several breaks for lemons and tea.

After 22 miles, the runners arrived at the foot of some steep climbs— "Heartbreak Hill"—in Newton. Here, Tom pulled ahead of Charlie, who eventually finished sixth. The *Boston Globe* reported that Tom smiled at the crowd as he raced and described him as "the most marvelous runner who has ever sped over our streets."

Tom ran the last mile of the marathon in 4 minutes 45 seconds (the world record for the mile was 4:15). He crossed the finish line with a time of 2:24:24—5 minutes ahead of the course record and three-quarters of a mile ahead of the second-place finisher— yet he still had plenty of energy. As spectators cheered him and threw hats, canes, and umbrellas

Tom posed with his trophies in 1907.

into the air, he moved onto an indoor track to run a few laps and walk several more.

Canadians welcomed Tom home with a victory parade. He rode in an open car adorned with a national flag to a celebration at Toronto's City Hall.

Many of Tom Longboat's training ideas were ahead of his time. Each day, he walked about 20 miles and lifted weights for an hour, and he limited long runs to two per week. After a big race or long training session, he rested.

Tom Longboat has been called the greatest marathon runner of all time. He died in 1949 at age 61, but his name lives on.

ON THE RUN

 Tom spent 4 years in the Canadian Army as a runner and message carrier during World War I. (People joked that he could outrun bullets.)

 The Longboat Roadrunners of Toronto formed in 1980 in honor of Tom. They hold an annual 10k race and award a scholarship at the University of Toronto to a Native Canadian who excels in running.

 In 1998, a Canadian magazine proclaimed Tom to be one of the 100 most important Canadians in history. In a category called "Stars," he was number one, ahead of hockey legend Wayne Gretzky and singer Celine Dion.

BACKYARD OLYMPICS

The next time you think that you have nothing to do, round up some other kids for a friendly competition. Or practice for the next neighborhood event by competing against yourself and trying to do better each time. Just follow the easy rules, and you'll be on the winners' platform!

YOU WILL NEED:

- 1 piece of paper (any kind, any size)
- 1 small stone or similar object per competitor
- 1 additional small stone or object
- 1 coin
- 1 stick of chalk, optional

OPTIONAL, FOR COMPETING AGAINST YOURSELF:

- digital watch or a clock with a seconds hand
- measuring stick or tape

The One Leg Hop

Hop on one foot as many times as possible. The highest count wins.

The Head Balance

Balance the stone or object on your head, while clapping your hands. All competitors start at the same time. Whoever does it the longest wins.

The Paper Throw

Stand at a permanent line (edge of the driveway, walkway, or the like) or draw a chalk line on the pavement. Crumple up the paper. Stand behind the line and, in turns, throw the paper. Mark your throw with your stone. The longest toss wins.

The One Leg Stand

Stand on one foot for as long as possible. All competitors start at the same time. The longest stand wins.

The Coin Toss

Designate one side of the coin as "heads." Each competitor, in turn, flips the coin 10 times. The person who tosses "heads" the most wins.

TO SCORE:

1. The top score in each event is the number of competitors. The next score is one less, and so forth. For example, if there are four kids playing, first place is worth 4 points, second is worth 3, third is worth 2, and fourth is worth 1.

2. In the event of a tie, average the scores involved. For example, if the top two of four finishers in The One Leg Hop each hopped 20 times before stopping, then the scores 4 and 3 would be averaged, and each of the top two finishers would get 3.5 points.

3. Add up the scores for all events to determine the overall winner.

- **To compete against yourself:** Count, time, or measure your performance in the events. Record the results and try to beat your score next time.

- **Multiplayer tiebreaker, or to really compete against yourself:** Use the "opposite" leg or arm from that used the first time. Omit The Head Balance and The Coin Toss.

The Paper Kick

Crumple up the piece of paper again. All competitors take turns kicking it from behind the same line. Mark each kick with the competitor's stone. The longest kick wins.

The Stone Throw

This is similar to the Italian game of bocce (BOTCH-ee). Toss or place the extra stone or object about 10 feet away. Competitors throw their own stone at it. The winning stone is the one that ends up closest to the first one without touching it.

GAME ON!

What games and challenges do you and your friends enjoy? Share them at Almanac4kids.com/tellus.

Rabbit Roundup

FURRY FRIENDS

OUR

- A male rabbit is called a **buck.**
- A female rabbit is called a **doe.**
- Rabbits usually give birth at night.
- When **kits,** or baby rabbits, are born, they weigh about 1 ounce.
- Any rabbit can be called a **bunny.** (It's like calling a cat a kitty.)
- A group of rabbits is called a **herd.**
- A group of baby rabbits is called a **litter,** or **nest.**

Rabbits have been around for thousands of years, but they were originally found only in Africa and Europe—and especially in Spain, where there was an early overabundance of the animal. That country's name comes from the Latin word *Hispania*, which means "the land of rabbits." Until about 400 years ago, rabbits were kept for food and fur. Then people started to keep them as pets, too.

Wild rabbits live in forests, thickets, meadows, prairies, and deserts, usually underground in clusters of burrows, called warrens, that are dug by does. A warren helps to protect rabbits from their enemies. Rabbits are prey to numerous predators, such as foxes, hawks, owls, wolves, and even raccoons. To escape danger, rabbits use their keen sense of smell and excellent hearing and eyesight (sometimes they sleep with their eyes open!). Rabbits' long, flexible ears are their best defense. They can detect even the slightest sounds.

Rabbits' hind legs, which are longer than their front legs, help them to hop up to 15 feet—and communicate. (More on that in a minute.) Fur padding on the bottoms of their hind feet helps to reduce the shock of landing after a leap.

Rabbits have sharp front teeth called incisors, plus peg teeth, which are additional incisors behind the front teeth. Peg teeth are used mainly for grabbing and cutting food. Being herbivores, rabbits feast on plants for food, usually preferring their sprouts and stems. They like clover, dandelions, and other weeds, as well as brussels sprouts, celery, grass, hay, herbs, oats, peppers, and, of course, carrots.

(continued)

In the winter, when food is in short supply, rabbits nibble on tender tree bark. After eating in the morning, rabbits produce mushy, partly digested droppings, which they eat. This provides them with extra nutrients.

When a rabbit is alarmed, it will warn other rabbits of the danger by thumping its hind feet. If a rabbit feels safe, it may lie on its stomach with its legs outstretched. If it screams or grinds its teeth loudly, it may be in pain, but quiet grinding usually signals contentment, much like a cat's purr.

JACKRABBIT

BELGIAN HARE

HARE, YE! HARE, YE!

Many people think that hares and rabbits are the same, but they are not. Hares are larger than rabbits and have longer legs and ears. When hare kits are born, they have a lot of fur and their eyes are open. When rabbit kits are born, they have no hair and their eyes and ears are sealed shut.

Confused? Here's more news: **Jackrabbits** are **hares** and the **Belgian hare** is a **rabbit!**

Man—er, Rabbit—in the Moon?

Many countries have a tale about what images appear in the full Moon. In Japan, people see a rabbit making *mochi* (a sticky rice cake) with a big wooden hammer.

TALES with TAILS

Match each rabbit with the clue to its story.

1. **Brer Rabbit**
2. **Peter Cottontail**
3. **Peter Rabbit**
4. **Thumper**
5. **Uncle Wiggily**
6. **Velveteen Rabbit**

a. rabbit gentleman

b. "creetur" known to Uncle Remus

c. gift to a boy at Christmas

d. friend to Jimmy Skunk, Johnny Chuck, Hooty Owl, and others

e. was chased out of Mr. McGregor's garden

f. friend of Flower and the wobbly-legged fawn, Bambi

Answers:
1. b; 2. d; 3. e; 4. f; 5. a; 6. c

LUCKY LORE

If someone wishes you "rabbit, rabbit, white rabbit" first thing in the morning on the first day of the month, say thank you. A common superstition holds that receiving this greeting bestows good luck for the rest of the month. The exact origin of the tradition is unknown, but it can be traced to 1420 in England.

PETICULARS

Q Why do cats purr?

A Cats purr when they are happy, when they are giving birth, or when they are injured or afraid. Scientists, who have measured the vibrations from a cat's purr, believe that the vibrations promote healing and help to increase bone strength. So, when your kitty purrs, she may be happy or she just may be giving herself a healing pep talk.

Q Do dogs and cats have good vision?

A Dogs and cats have better night vision than humans. Underneath the retina is a special reflective layer that helps them to see in dim light. This is the reason that their eyes shine when they face a bright source of light, such as a car's headlights, at night. Because most dogs' eyes are on the sides of their head, their peripheral vision (sight on the side) is greater than ours. While dogs  and cats are not able to see all of the colors that we see, they do see shades of red and blue.

Itching to Know About Fleas?

Fleas can pull 160,000 times their own weight.

Cat and dog fleas are very similar. Cat fleas are more common in North America and are found on both cats and dogs.

Fleas can jump 150 times their own length, vertically or horizontally. This is equivalent to a human jumping about 1,000 feet.

Fleas live about 2 to 3 months, on average.

As carriers of plague, fleas have killed more people than have died in all of the wars ever fought.

Fleas are covered with bristles and spines that point backward. (This is why it is difficult to pick a flea from your pet's fur.)

Fleas do not have ears and are virtually blind.

Fleas can jump 30,000 times without stopping, and every time they jump, they reverse direction.

Tiny bits of black dirt on your pet's bedding are flea poop and an indication that fleas are present.

To free a pet of fleas, give it a thorough shampoo, lathering for 15 minutes, and then rinse and dry. You may have to repeat this several times. If you can't get rid of the fleas yourself, contact your vet. Clean the bedding and vacuum any part of the house that the pet has been in.

Meet some awesome animals with uncommon talents.

PETS AT WORK

I'm a Paso Fino horse. Painting is my passion. My full name is Castillo de Paradiso, but my friends call me ROMEO.

My job: I've been painting since 2004. My partner, Cheryl Ward, prepares the canvas, picks the colors, dips my brush, and rotates the frame. I hold the brush in my mouth and paint with bold strokes. We can finish a 3x3-foot painting in about 15 minutes.

My story: I was shy before I started painting with Cheryl. We paint in our outdoor studio in Floral City, Florida, and at fairs and exhibitions. Some paintings have sold for $2,500!

I love that I'm not haltered or tied, I can walk away at any time, and I get Cheryl's undivided attention, plus carrots and alfalfa bits after every few brush strokes.

I loathe washing my face on a rag that Cheryl holds for me, posing for photos, and sharing easel time.

They call me 92 or **MR. RELIABLE.** I'm a racing homing pigeon, and someday I'll become a coach.

My job: I fly for Rocky Mountain Adventures in Fort Collins, Colorado. I wear an aerodynamic backpack, and I deliver digital photos of vacationing river rafters back to the main office so that prints can be made for them. I do two gigs a week in a 3-month season. I get August off. It's hawk migratory season—very risky!

My story: I learned the routes from my parents. I trained with them on short flights and worked up to full flights on my own.

I love that even when I'm off duty, I can go out a couple of times a day for 30-minute laps above the house. Off-season, I do flights as long as 150 miles.

I loathe the time pressure (no dillydallying!) and the danger. At top speed, about 60 mph, I can outfly most predators if I see them coming. If I don't, it will be lights out for me.

continued ● ● ● ● ➡

I'm NEOS, the cat. I work as a library ambassador and stress-relief therapist. Oh— I also catch mice.

Security guard GABRIEL here. I'm more antisocial than most llamas, but this makes me good at my job.

My job: I tend more than three dozen ewes on the Isle of Skye Farm, near Brooks, Alberta. I graze with the flock to keep it safe from coyotes, dogs, even cows and horses.

My story: The sheep know that I'm the leader in the pasture and I'll protect them. I once ran a coyote out of the field.

I love newborn lambs. I even skip around the pasture with them.

I loathe people. Sometimes they can't be avoided, like when I need an inoculation, but I put up a fuss.

My job: I work at the NAIT College Library in Fairview, Alberta. It's warm and quiet, perfect for snoozing—and it's okay if I sleep on the job.

My story: I was rescued by the college's Animal Health department. Now my room, board, veterinary care, and library membership are free.

I love the attention that I get from the students, walking the 20-foot-high railing along the library's mezzanine, and the week off at Christmas with a former staff member. Her home is like my personal resort.

I loathe the long hours—I work 24/7/365, except for that one week off.

Working Wonders

For centuries, humans have relied on animals to help them. Today, there are lots of "jobs" for animals. Here are a few:

- **Dogs** serve as baggage sniffers and hotel concierges, track pythons in the Everglades, predict when their human "partner" might have a seizure, and jump out of helicopters to rescue swimmers in distress.

- **Falcons** protect vineyards from songbirds and keep seagulls out of dumps and away from airports.

- **Geese** guard large companies and warehouses from intruders (the geese honk if they're disturbed).

- **Miniature horses** serve as guides for visually impaired people.

Does your pet work?
Tell us about it at
Almanac4kids.com/tellus.

SPILLING THE Beans ABOUT Chocolate

People have been crazy for cocoa for centuries.

hocolate grows on cacao trees. These colorful trees can reach up to 30 feet tall and are grown on independent and cooperative farms in tropical rain forests. Each cacao tree produces flowers and football-size pods that turn red, yellow, or orange when they are ripe. Each pod contains 20 to 60 cacao beans. At harvesttime, the beans are scooped out, fermented for about a week, and then dried in the sun.

Football-size pods grow on a cacao tree in Sri Lanka, Asia. Above are pods that have been harvested.

Later, at a factory, the beans are roasted before finally being crushed into a paste that is used to make chocolate. About 400 beans are needed to make 1 pound of chocolate!

To make sweet chocolate, cacao bean paste is mixed in vats with condensed milk, sugar, and extra cocoa butter (a vegetable fat by-product). The result is a gritty mixture that is smoothed out in a different machine. Finally, paste is "conched," or heated, kneaded, and churned.

When the chocolate is ready, it is poured into molds and then cooled, wrapped, and packaged.

The scientific name of the cacao tree, *Theobroma cacao,* means "food of the gods." *Cacao* is the early Spanish word for "cocoa."

CONTINUED • • • • • • • •

MELTING THROUGH

The ancient Aztecs used cacao beans like money. A turkey hen was worth 100 beans, a turkey egg was worth three beans, and a large tomato cost one bean. • • • • • •

On August 15, 1502, Christopher Columbus found some cacao beans in a dugout canoe near what is now Honduras. He took some back to Europe, but no one knew what to do with them. •

Around 1517, Spanish explorer Hernando Cortés tasted cacao, liked it, and called it "chocolat" because he had difficulty in pronouncing its Aztec name, *xocolatl.* • • • • • • •

• • • • The first solid-chocolate candy bar was made in 1847.

The first milk-chocolate candy appeared in 1875. • • • • • • • • • • • •

Sweet Science

Some people say that eating chocolate makes them feel good. This may be because chocolate contains over 300 chemicals and stimulants.

Chocolate melts at about 98°F. That's lower than the temperature of the human body (98.6°F) and explains why chocolate melts in your mouth.

F
O
O
D

IME

 In 1911, during their "race" to reach the South Pole, Roald Amundsen and Robert Falcon Scott both ate chocolate. • • •

One day in the 1930s, Ruth Wakefield, owner of the Toll House Inn in Whitman, Massachusetts, was making cookies. She cut up a chocolate bar and added the pieces to the dough. She thought that the chips would melt into the batter. They didn't, and the "chocolate chip" cookie was born! • • •

In 1953, the first people to climb Mount Everest, Edmund Hillary and Tenzing Norgay, celebrated with a chocolate bar at the top. But they didn't eat the candy. Norgay buried it in the snow, as a tribute to the gods of the mountain. • • • • •

In 1969, the *Apollo 11* astronauts brought packages of dehydrated, freeze-dried, chocolate pudding to the Moon.

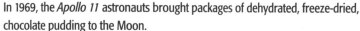

Chocolate can be poison to some pets, such as dogs, cats, and birds, depending on how much is eaten. Play it safe and don't give your pets chocolate.

Chocolate extracts are used in shampoo, cosmetics, soap, lip gloss, lotion, and scented candles.

Find out where Roald Dahl got his idea for *Charlie and the Chocolate Factory*, plus more, at Almanac4kids.com/chocolate.

A SLICE of

Pizza is not Italian (well, not entirel

Ancient Egyptians (c. 3000 B.C.) celebrated the birthdays of pharaohs with unleavened bread (like pita) covered with herbs.

Soldiers in Persia (c. 500 B.C.) baked thin bread on their shields and then topped the bread with cheese and dates.

Roman historian **Cato the Elder (234–149 B.C.)** wrote about eating "flat rounds of dough dressed with olive oil, herbs, and honey baked on stones."

In 1522, Spanish explorers returned home from the New World with tomatoes. Wealthy people believed that the fruits were poisonous. Only peasants were brave (and hungry) enough to eat them.

At the same time, peasants in Naples, Italy, were making and eating flat bread almost every day, occasionally topping the bread with tomatoes. Soon, word spread that these breads were the best in all of Italy.

By 1889, Italian peasants had added herbs and cheese to their flat breads. When their queen, Margherita, visited, she wanted to taste this delicacy and summoned chef Raffaele Esposito to make it for her. (Royalty did not like to be seen eating peasant food.)

CONTINUED

nd it wasn't invented. It evolved . . .

TOP THIS!

- The largest round pizza, made in South Africa in 1990, measured 122 feet 8 inches and contained 3,968 pounds of cheese and 1,984 pounds of tomato sauce.

- The largest rectangular pizza, made in Iowa in 2005, measured 129 by 98 feet and contained 4,000 pounds of cheese and 700 pounds of tomato sauce.

Raffaele made three pizzas: one with pork fat, cheese, and basil; one with garlic, olive oil, and tomatoes; and one with tomatoes, cheese, and basil (red, white, and green in honor of the Italian flag). The queen's favorite was the last, so Raffaele named it Pizza Margherita.

The idea of pizza as a meal spread slowly. The first licensed pizzeria in the United States, Lombardi's, opened in the "Little Italy" section of New York City in 1905. **In the late 1940s,** when soldiers who had been in Italy during World War II returned home craving tomato pies like they had eaten in Italy, they found them at Lombardi's.

Soon, **pizzerias were everywhere,** and today, pizza is enjoyed around the world.

What's Your Pizza Personality?

ACCORDING TO RESEARCHERS . . .

kids who like . . .	are . . .
pineapple and other nontraditional toppings	leaders and high achievers
one meat	arguers and procrastinators
several meats	the center of attention and always look presentable
one veggie	understanding and easygoing
several veggies	honest and reliable

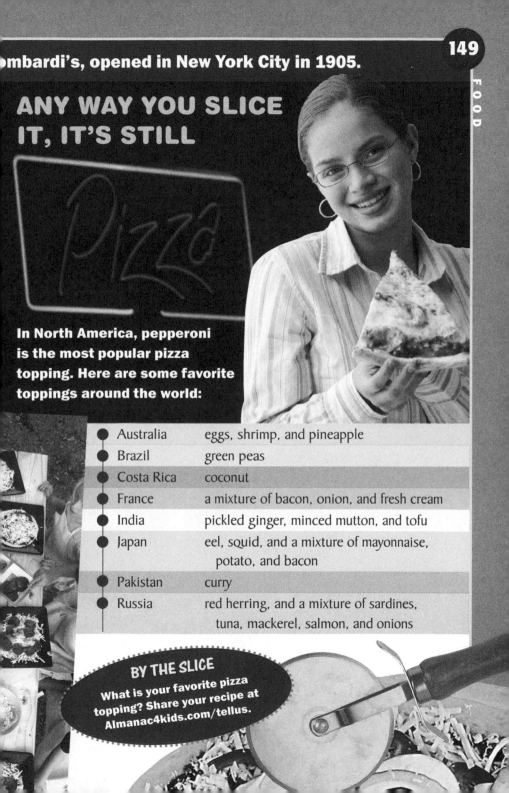

F
O
O
D

mbardi's, opened in New York City in 1905.

ANY WAY YOU SLICE IT, IT'S STILL

Pizza

In North America, pepperoni is the most popular pizza topping. Here are some favorite toppings around the world:

Australia	eggs, shrimp, and pineapple
Brazil	green peas
Costa Rica	coconut
France	a mixture of bacon, onion, and fresh cream
India	pickled ginger, minced mutton, and tofu
Japan	eel, squid, and a mixture of mayonnaise, potato, and bacon
Pakistan	curry
Russia	red herring, and a mixture of sardines, tuna, mackerel, salmon, and onions

BY THE SLICE

What is your favorite pizza topping? Share your recipe at Almanac4kids.com/tellus.

Honey, EAT YOUR ANTS!

There are over 1,400 species of edible insects in the world. In many countries, they are common snacks. The practice of eating insects is called **entomophagy**.

- Folks in 36 African countries munch on at least 537 different insects.

- Street vendors in Thailand sell fried grasshoppers, beetles, and other bugs.

- In China, people eat fried caterpillars and silkworm pupae.

- Worm crisp, chocolate-covered scorpions, crispy crickets, and ant lollipops are available year-round from a gourmet shop in London.

- Fried grasshoppers prepared with garlic, salt, lime juice, or a red chili powder coating are popular in some parts of Mexico.

- "Big-bottomed ants," or *Hormiga culona,* toasted, are eaten by folks in northern Colombia.

- Diners in a Santa Monica, California, restaurant can order chicken-stuffed water bugs and Thai-style white sea worms.

- In Sardinia, Italy, there's a special cheese called *casu marzu,* or "rotten cheese," because it contains live maggots, or fly larvae.

grasshopper

cricket

ants

beetle

maggots

scorpion

MORE

FAVORITE BUGS	WHERE
Caterpillars	China, Mexico
Giant water bugs	Asia
Grubs	Papua New Guinea
Katydids	Philippines
Locusts	Africa, South Korea
Termites	Africa, Australia

termites   katydid

☞ **WHY EAT BUGS?** They can be good for you! Some insects have twice the protein of raw meat and fish. They contain less fat than most junk food and even healthy food like some meats. Some bugs have important minerals and vitamins. When cooked and prepared correctly, they're no more likely to carry germs or disease than are meat or fish.

You probably already eat insects. When farm crops are processed, a certain number of insects or insect parts get mixed into peanut butter, spaghetti sauce, and other foods. The U.S. Food and Drug Administration knows this and allows small amounts to be present. Most people unknowingly eat a pound or two of insects each year.

Need a Boost? Drink
BUG JUICE!

■ In the 2000 Summer Olympics, Naoko Takahashi of Japan won the women's marathon, becoming the first Japanese woman to win an Olympic gold medal. She says that drinking the stomach juices of Asian giant hornets gave her extra energy for the long race.

■ Scientists in Japan had been studying Asian giant hornets, trying to figure out how they can fly distances equal to two marathons (26 miles 385 yards, doubled) in one day while hunting for food. The scientists determined that acidic juices in the hornets' stomachs help them to convert fat to energy so that they can fly far. Scientists fed the juice to mice, who were also able to run longer and faster. A Japanese company is now making an energy drink out of this juice.

Asian giant hornet

Say WHAT?

Crickets use organs in their knees to listen. Fish respond to sound through ridges on their bodies, and snakes use their tongues. Humans, of course, have ears.

How Ears Work

THE OUTER EAR—the part you see—catches sound waves. It's shaped like a funnel, catching noise and sending it down the ear canal to the eardrum. Sound waves cause the eardrum to vibrate. Three small bones in the middle ear then pass these vibrations on to the cochlea, a fluid-filled structure of the inner ear. The cochlea contains liquid that moves like a wave in response to sounds. The cochlea is also lined with microscopic hairs that move, creating nerve signals that are sent to the brain, which makes sense of the sounds we hear.

FACTS WAX

The skin cells of the outer ear contain tiny glands that produce wax that protects the ears by trapping dirt and other things in the ear. The wax slowly works its way out of the ear.

ANATOMY OF THE EAR

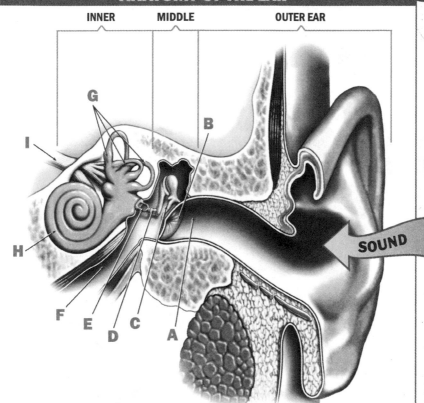

INNER · MIDDLE · OUTER EAR

SOUND

A external auditory canal
B eardrum
C hammer
D anvil
E stapes (stirrup)

F eustachian tube
G semicircular canals that house the
receptors for equilibrium
H cochlea (houses the receptors for hearing)
I nerve that transmits impulses to the brain

The hammer, anvil, and stirrup pass along vibrations.

approx.
actual size

Did You Know?

The smallest bone in the human body is the stapes, or stirrup. It's 0.10 to 0.13 inch long and weighs 1.9 to 4.3 milligrams.

continued

You have two, but one will never work as well as the pair.

➡ Never play your headset volume too loud.

In a Dizzy Daze

■ Have you ever felt dizzy after spinning? Three small loops in your inner ear called semicircular canals are filled with fluid and covered with microscopic hairs, just like the cochlea. Whenever you move your head, the fluid in these canals moves, too. Spinning makes you dizzy because the fluid in the canals continues to spin after you stop. You feel dizzy until the fluid stops moving.

Can't Stop the Pop

■ Whenever you change altitude (fly in an airplane or travel a mountain road), the air pressure inside your ear changes. This pressure is regulated by the eustachian tube, which connects the middle ear with the back of the nose. This tube helps to equalize pressure on both sides of the eardrum. Whenever it opens, you hear a pop.

Heard Any Good Earworms Lately?

■ Don't be alarmed! An earworm is not an insect; it's a song such as "Who Let the Dogs Out?," "YMCA," or "It's a Small World After All" that you can't get out of your head once you hear it. The term comes from the German word for the problem, *Ohrwurm*.

Shore It Is . . .

■ The next time you're at the ocean, hold a large seashell to your ear. People say that you'll hear ocean waves or the blood traveling in your ears. Wrong! You hear the sounds around you bouncing off the inside of the shell.

➡ Wear earplugs or special earmuffs when you're around loud noises.

➡ Never put anything—a cotton swab, pen, or pencil, for instance—in your ear. You could puncture your eardrum.

continued

DEAF-DEFYING
Success Stories

◄ Composer **Ludwig van Beethoven** (1770–1827) began to lose his hearing at age 30. At the premiere of his 9th Symphony, he had to be turned around to face the audience because he couldn't hear the applause.

► Inventor **Thomas Edison** (1847–1931) became partly deaf as a teenager, probably the result of illnesses. He said that his deafness helped him to concentrate.

◄ The founder of the Girl Scouts, **Juliette Low** (1860–1927), suffered from chronic ear infections, causing hearing loss in one ear. She lost hearing in her other ear at her wedding, when a piece of good-luck rice was thrown and landed in her ear. It punctured her eardrum and caused an infection.

► Baseball center fielder **William Ellsworth "Dummy" Hoy** (1862–1961) was left deaf by a childhood illness. He taught his teammates sign language and helped to pioneer the use of the many hand signals still used in baseball today.

◄ As a toddler, **Helen Keller** (1880–1968) was left blind and deaf by illness. She became the first blind and deaf person to graduate from college.

► Actress **Marlee Matlin** (b. 1965) lost her hearing after a childhood illness. She went on to become the first deaf actress to win an Academy Award, as Best Actress, for the 1986 film *Children of a Lesser God*.

Quick Fixes

Before there were so many lotions and ointments in stores, people relied on commonsense cures. These remedies were recommended in the 1800s:

◆ If you cut yourself while cooking, apply molasses to the wound to bind it temporarily.

◆ For relief from a toothache, apply a poultice of gingerroot to your cheek on the side of the tooth pain.

◆ For a sudden attack of croup, bathe your neck with bear, goose, or any kind of oily animal grease.

◆ Clip an ingrown toenail as near to the flesh as possible. When the corner of the nail can be raised up, put a tuft of fine lint under it.

◆ Have parched or chapped lips and no lip balm handy? Massage your mouth with a dab of earwax—preferably your own.

◆ To soothe a strained muscle, rub an ointment made from common earthworms on the swollen area.

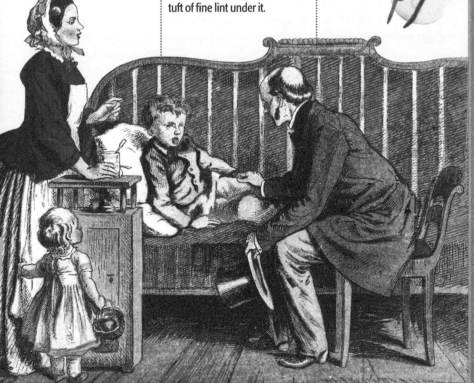

The Man With the See

O n June 6, 1822, Dr. William Beaumont was summoned to treat 19-year-old French-Canadian fur trapper Alexis St. Martin near Fort Mackinac in the Michigan Territory. Alexis had been accidentally shot in the stomach by a friend's shotgun. The duck shot (small pellets) from the gun had struck the trapper's abdomen, blowing a hole (fistula) of several inches in diameter in his stomach.

Using primitive tools, Dr. Beaumont carefully dressed the wound. He did not expect Alexis to live more than about 36 hours. Neither, however, did the doctor fully appreciate his own skill or know the strength and determination of his patient.

One year later, Alexis was still alive. The wound had healed, except for a small hole that had to be covered with a compress and bandage to prevent food and drink from coming out. Gradually, a flap of skin grew over the hole. Dr. Beaumont was surprised and excited. At the time, very little was known about how the human stomach functions, and the doctor saw the unusual wound as an opportunity to learn.

The curious doctor and his incredible patient began a series of experiments in 1825. At specific times each afternoon, as Alexis lay on his side, Dr. Beaumont would suspend food that was tied to a silk string into the hole in Alexis's stomach. He would watch it be digested and then record what he observed. Some foods tested included beef, pork, chicken, stale bread, and raw cabbage.

After two months, Alexis, who endured headaches and indigestion through it all, lost patience and fled to Canada. There, he married and started a family.

Four years later, Dr. Beaumont contacted Alexis and offered to pay him to continue the experiments. Needing money, Alexis agreed, but by 1833 he had returned to Canada for good. He lived to be in his 80s.

In all, Dr. Beaumont conducted over 200 different experiments on Alexis. His observations became the basis for a book (*Experiments and Observations on the Gastric Juice, and the Physiology of Digestion*) that is still considered one of the most authoritative works on gastric action.

hrough Stomach

> What is food to one man may be fierce poison to others.
>
> –*Lucretius, Roman poet (95–55 B.C.)*

Army surgeon William Beaumont collects gastric juice from his patient, Alexis St. Martin, during a routine experiment.

Hairs to You!

Some facts to comb through

Hair is the only human body part that continually grows, degenerates, and grows again throughout life.

All body hairs grow at about the same rate—about ½-inch per month. (Eyelashes and forearm hairs usually fall out before then.) The hair on your head grows for 2 to 6 years before it withers at its base and falls out. We each shed 50 to 80 hairs a day—more in the spring and fall. Hair follicles on your scalp rest for about 3 months and then start growing new hairs.

The shape of the follicle determines whether you have straight, wavy, or curly hair. A hair shaft can be round, oval, or flat.

Hair color comes from the pigment melanin, which also colors your skin and eyes. Gray hair is not really gray, but has a lack of pigment in the hair shaft, making it white or opaque.

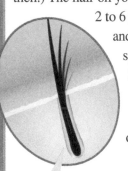

A hair grows from its follicle in stages.

FOR HEALTHY HAIR

Eat a well-balanced diet.

Brush hair when it is dry; twice a day is best.

Use a wide-tooth comb, not a brush, on wet hair.

Brush hair to distribute natural oils and add sheen.

Expect rain if curly hair gets curlier and straight hair gets straighter.
—folklore

SPLITTING HAIRS

Blondes have about 140,000 hairs.

Brunettes have about 105,000 hairs.

edheads have about),000 hairs.

HUES NEWS

To color their hair around 1200 B.C., Egyptians used indigo (for blue-violet), leaves from the henna bush (for red), or dried tadpoles from a canal crushed in oil (for reasons we do not understand). These days, it's much easier to add highlights with items from the pantry.

To enhance the color of blond hair, add lemon juice or white vinegar to the rinse water.

To enhance the color of brown or black hair, add cider vinegar to the rinse water.

To add reddish highlights to blond or light brown hair, rinse it with hibiscus tea.

CUTS FOR KIDS

♥ Children who experience medical hair loss appreciate having a natural-hair wig to wear. If your hair is at least 10 inches long, you may be able to donate it to www.locksoflove.org.

SLOWPOKE'S
Last-Place Win

ears before automobiles ruled the roads, horsepower was truly of the four-legged kind. Almost every farmer raised horses, and fast ones were prized. That's why, in 1910, the slow horse race at the Brattleboro Fair in Vermont caused a whirlwind of curiosity and excitement.

A prize of $25 was offered to the horse and driver that could take up the most time going around the half-mile track trotting all the while and pulling any two-wheeled vehicle.

On race day, 20 horses stood at the starting line. Some were plump, young, and healthy. Others were skinny and showing their age. They and their owners had come from Vermont, New Hampshire, and Massachusetts. Farmer Wilmont, from Ludlow, Vermont, sat behind his swayback named Slowpoke. "He's a good hoss," Farmer Wilmont told the crowd of spectators. "He belongs to the Sooner breed. He'd sooner stand than go."

When the starting bell sounded, the surprised horses stepped lively from the line and the drivers, each in a vehicle behind, had to slow them.

Farmer Wilmont shouted at Slowpoke, "Get a-going, Slowpoke, you'll never make it around." Slowpoke maintained a trot, but his feet had a way of coming down almost in the same place from which they had come up. He advanced very little.

FINISH LINE

"Cheer up, old boy!" Wilmont cried out. "You just might make it."

By halfway around the track, about half of the drivers had given up their chase. Their horses had begun acting up or wouldn't keep the required pace. Any horse that walked was automatically removed from the race. Slowpoke swished his tail and dogtrotted along.

When the last horse passed Slowpoke, Wilmont yelled, "Tell the judge I hope to make it there—someday!"

Slowpoke did make it, and it wasn't even a close finish. Slowpoke was at least 200 feet behind the second-slowest horse. The horse race judge and fair officials declared Slowpoke the winner, proof that being slow and steady can win the race.

Gait Guide

Horses have different gaits, or ways of moving. A horse's actual speed depends on its breed, build, stride length, and other factors.

A **WALK** is a four-beat gait in which each leg lands separately.

A **TROT** is a two-beat gait in which the legs move and land in diagonal pairs.

A **CANTER** is a three-beat gait, similar to a slow gallop, in which first the outside hind leg, then the inside hind leg and outside foreleg together, then the inside foreleg land in sequence.

A **GALLOP** is a fast, natural, three-beat gait.

The KID Who Invented

If it weren't for Philo T. Farnsworth, inventor of television, we'd st

Philo T. Farnsworth was born in a log cabin at Indian Creek, near Beaver, Utah, in 1906. As a boy he was fascinated by anything electrical or mechanical, and he loved talking with his father about the workings of locomotives, radios, or the family's hand-crank telephone. Philo thought that it would be fun to make things, and by the age of 6 he had declared that he would be an inventor when he grew up.

In 1919, Philo and his family moved to a ranch in Idaho. There he found forgotten treasure in the house's attic: a stack of science magazines. He spent hours reading them, as well as anything else about science or inventions that he could find. Thomas Edison, Alexander Graham Bell, and other inventors became his heroes.

Philo constantly looked for ways to put his knowledge to use. When he discovered that the ranch's electrical system didn't work, he studied the manual, took the system apart, and repaired it all by himself. He built motors for his mother's manual washing and sewing machines so that they would run on electricity, and he won a national award for developing a theft-proof ignition switch for cars.

In January 1930, Philo demonstrates his all-electronic television receiver.

Living on a farm meant that Philo had chores to do, such as tending sheep and helping his father with the crops. Inventions were never far from his mind, however. Once, when he was plowing a potato field, Philo was thinking about a new machine that he'd read about—the television.

TV

eating frozen radio dinners.

–Johnny Carson, American TV host (1925–2005)

Televisions of the time transmitted images using mechanical disks and mirrors, but the images were blurry and could not be broadcast very far. When Philo looked

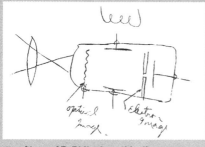

At age 15, Philo drew this diagram to explain his idea to his chemistry teacher, Justin Tolman.

at the evenly spaced rows he had been plowing, he had an idea. He realized that a television image could be transmitted in much the same way—by scanning a picture one row at a time, from side to side. Instead of depending on moving parts, he thought, television transmitters could send images to a receiver by converting them to electricity first. The receiver would convert the signal to a beam of electrons (charged particles) that could be shot at a fluorescent tube that

would "reassemble" them into a picture, even at great distances.

Later, at school (a 4-mile ride on horseback), Philo drew a diagram of his "image dissector" on a notebook page for his chemistry teacher. The instructor was impressed but admitted that even he couldn't totally understand Philo's complex idea.

A picture of Joan Crawford appears on the cathode-ray tube after being televised from an adjoining room at a demonstration at the Franklin Institute in Philadelphia, Pennsylvania, 1934.

(continued)

Philo was curious and always enjoyed learning things. Good study habits helped him to be admitted to Brigham Young University in 1924. Two years later, when his father died, he had to leave school to support his family. He took a variety of odd jobs but never gave up on his dream of being an inventor.

One day, while stuffing envelopes at a marketing company, Philo described his idea for the image dissector to his employers. They were so excited by its possibilities that they offered him money to test his idea. Philo set up a laboratory in San Francisco and went to work, often becoming so absorbed in what he was doing that he would forget to eat.

Finally, on September 7, 1927, Philo was ready to test the image dissector. He

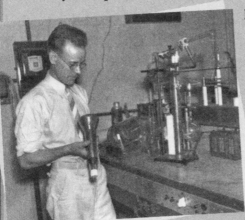

placed a glass plate with a line scratched in it in front of a camera lens. With his two investors and his wife looking on, Philo flicked a switch. Suddenly, they could see the line on a glass receiver tube in the next room. "There you have it," Philo announced proudly. "Electronic television."

In May 1928, Philo transmitted an image of his wife to a receiver in front of an audience. Over the next several years, he patented ten

In July 1935, Philo examines components for an early television. The image dissector in his left hand is his own invention.

processes that advanced TV technology. However, he soon learned that big companies such as RCA were better able to manufacture and market televisions than he, a lone inventor, was.

By the 1940s, his role as the inventor of modern television was largely forgotten. The lack of fame and fortune didn't bother Philo, who told his wife, "We have too much to do for the future to worry about it." He was happy to keep inventing, and he turned his amazingly creative mind to other projects. Among the devices he invented were . . .

- a forerunner to radar
- an infrared telescope
- the first incubator for premature babies
- an air-traffic control system
- the first electron microscope

By the end of his life in 1971, Philo T. Farnsworth had been credited with more than 300 patents, achieving the goal he had set for himself at age 6.

HOW TO GET RICH
Without Doing Any Work

Folk beliefs about money have been around for thousands of years because some people would rather wish for riches than work for them. What those people don't tell you is that some of these methods can be very difficult!

Throw a feather over a house, run around to the other side, and catch it before it hits the ground.

Dream of a white horse.

When your left palm itches, rub it on wood and put the hand into your pocket.

When you see a shooting star, say "Money, money, money" before the star goes out.

Get a buzzard to land on your house on a **MONDAY.**

Touch the money in your pocket whenever you hear a whippoorwill (a very well camouflaged bird).

DON'T MOVE CATS.

WEAR RED CLOTHES.

Swallow a raw chicken heart. (Yuck!)

Always cut your fingernails on **TUESDAY.**

Wear one pant leg tucked into a boot and one pant leg out.

LET A SPIDER CRAWL OVER YOU.

DREAMWORK
What kind of work do you want to do when you grow up? Tell other kids at Almanac4kids.com/tellus.

The Toughest Cowboy

Nobody knows his real name, where he came from, or why he died, but he's still with us.

LVESTER'S SECRET

SYLVESTER

Ever

Body of Evidence

In 1895, in the Gila Bend Desert of Arizona, two cowboys found a naked body that had been shot dead by a bullet to the stomach. They pulled the body from the sand and took it to Yuma for identification. All such efforts failed, so somebody nicknamed the body "Sylvester."

For a while, Sylvester sat propped up in the corner of a secondhand store in Yuma. Then he went on tour.

He was featured as an attraction at carnivals in Texas and as a curiosity in sideshows in the Midwest. He horrified visitors to the Alaska–Yukon Exposition in Seattle in 1909, stunned audiences at the Panama–Pacific Exposition in San Francisco in 1915, and baffled a curator at a museum on the East Coast.

When the public's appetite for such sideshows diminished, Sylvester was bumped from owner to owner. Finally, in 1955, the widow of one of the cowboys who had found Sylvester offered him to Ye Olde Curiosity Shop in Seattle, Washington. He has been there ever since.

Sylvester is a genuine mummy. Scientists have called him a perfect example of natural dehydration. Some experts claim that the combination of hot alkaline sand and dry desert air mummified Sylvester's body within 24 hours of his death. Other sources suggest that Sylvester had been preserved with arsenic in order to be displayed at sideshows. (The use of arsenic for such purposes ceased around 1900.)

Although gaunt and shrunken, the body is perfect in every detail. Hair, mustache, teeth, nails, blue eyes, organs—even the bloodstains from his fatal wounds—are preserved and intact.

Experts have concluded that 6-foot-tall Sylvester weighed about 225 when he died and was about 45 years old. The day of his death must have been one of high heat and low humidity, because his weight quickly dropped to 137 pounds and his skin became dark and leathery—just as it is today.

BIGFOOT or BIG FAKE?

For over a hundred years, in many different places, people have claimed sightings of a large, mysterious creature that looks to be part man, part ape. In North America, it's often called **BIGFOOT** or **SASQUATCH.**

Generations of native tribes in the Pacific Northwest and Canada have passed along stories about the scary beast. Some people even believe that 2,000 to 6,000 of them live in the wildernesses of North America. In most accounts, Bigfoot is about 8 feet tall and weighs over 500 pounds. It is said to have a shy personality and to like to sleep. According to one theory, it is an extinct giant ape called *Gigantopithecus*. Another hypothesis is that it is descended from an Asian ape that traveled to North America during the Ice Age.

Many people search for this creature, leading expeditions around the world. But nobody knows whether Bigfoot actually exists! Some people claim to have taken photos and video of Bigfoot, but no one has ever produced any authentic Bigfoot bones, scat (or poop), fur, footprints, or bodies.

SASQUATCH

Canadian teacher J. W. Burns came up with the name "Sasquatch" in the 1920s. While studying Native American accounts of Bigfoot, he noticed that many of the native names sounded alike, so he invented a new name to try to blend the similar ones. Now Burns's term is used by many people, especially those in the Northwest.

CONTINUED

WHAT'S HIS NAME?

Different cultures have different names for mysterious big-footed creatures. Here are a few:

NAME	PLACE
Hibagon	Japan
Kapre	Philippines
Karakoncolos	Turkey; Bulgaria
Momo the Monster	Missouri
Skunk Ape	Florida Everglades
Woolly Booger	Louisiana
Yeren	Hubei, China
Yeti	Tibet
Yowie	Australia

TRUTH OR DARE?

Roger Patterson and Bob Gimlin claimed that they caught Bigfoot on film on October 20, 1967, in northern California. The shaky footage, less than a minute long, shows a large, apelike creature walking through the woods. Later, a man claimed that he was the creature  in a costume. He said that the filmmakers had promised to pay him but never did. Some people think that this man is lying and that the animal in the tape is really Bigfoot.

CRYPTOZOOLOGY: the study of hidden or unknown animals, especially legendary ones such as Bigfoot.

BIGFOOT
FALSE ALARMS

In August 1958, in Humboldt, California, the local newspaper ran a story with a photograph of a plaster cast of a giant footprint found where a road was being built. The story and photo were reprinted in newspapers around the world.

It turns out that the giant footprints were made by Ray Wallace, whose company was building the road.

Ray kept the Bigfoot story going for years. In 1995, for instance, he claimed to have discovered that Bigfoot loved Kellogg's Frosted Flakes cereal. In 1998, he offered to pay $1 million to anyone who brought him a baby Bigfoot. (He wanted to teach the creature to do chores on his ranch.)

After Ray died in 2002, his children announced that their father had used a pair of carved wooden feet to make the footprints.

Sir Edmund Hillary, the New Zealand explorer who first climbed Mt. Everest in 1953, was part of a team searching for yetis in the Himalayan Mountains in 1960. The team searched for 10 months (Edmund became ill and had to leave early) and brought back three skin samples that they believed could have come from the yeti.

A view of the Himalayas

Scientific analysis proved that two of the samples were from bears and the other was from a goat.

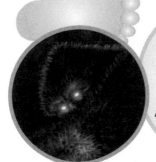

BIG OPINIONS
Do you think that Bigfoot is real? Why or why not? What name would you give it? Share your ideas with other kids at Almanac4kids.com/tellus.

Crash

THE
Worst-Ever
ON-PURPOSE
ACCIDENT

n the late 1800s, trains were crashed for entertainment—but it wasn't always fun.

In Cleveland, Ohio, in 1895, about 40,000 people watched the collision of two locomotives, each pulling freight cars. One of those spectators, William George Crush, became disappointed when the engines only bumped cowcatcher bars. Then and there, he decided to stage a crash that would be a smashing success.

William worked for the Missouri, Kansas, & Texas Railroad as a passenger agent in Texas. When he told his bosses about his idea for a "monster crash," they liked it immediately. They scheduled it for 4 P.M. on September 15, 1896, and put William in charge. They also provided two 35-ton locomotives in perfect working condition, plus 12 boxcars—six for each engine. One of the

Crush

The two stationary trains were posed for a "before" photo. They were then backed up, given the signal to start, and photographed again at the moment of collision.

engines, Number 999, was painted bright green. The other, Number 1001, was painted bright red. The boxcars were decorated and loaded with cross ties for additional weight.

Officials decided to stage the crash near Waco, Texas, where small hills rose up on three sides of a shallow valley. This terrain would give the trains a gravity-aided rolling start and the spectators a safe viewing place. The spot was named Crush, after the man with the plan.

Thousands of flyers advertising the event were posted all over Texas. Four miles of track was laid for the trains, and a grandstand, bandstand, reporters' platform, two telegraph offices, and depot were built. A circus tent was set up, inside which a restaurant served food.

☞ (continued)

The ground shook as boilers exploded and cars stacked up and derailed. Wood and steel fragments rained down on the terrified crowd. The locomotives were demolished, and many people suffered injuries.

On the appointed day, men, women, and children began arriving at dawn. Most had traveled by train. (Round-trip train tickets to the site from anywhere in Texas were $2 each.) Some of the coaches were so full that a few passengers sat on the roof.

By midafternoon, more than 40,000 people had crowded into the valley. They passed the time picnicking, enjoying the games and shows of a carnival that had set up, and listening to people giving speeches.

The two trains stood at opposite ends of the track belching smoke and soot. In the valley, midway between them, stood a telegraph pole. The sign on it read "Point of Collision."

At 5 P.M., one hour late, the locomotives rolled toward the telegraph pole so that a photograph of the crews could be taken. Then they slowly returned to their starting positions.

Ten minutes later, William, on horseback, rose and waved his hat, signaling the start of the event. Cheers rang out from the crowd, as many people stood on tiptoe to watch.

No one could have predicted what would happen next.

A report in the *Dallas Morning News* the next day describes great black streaks of smoke from the locomotives' funnels, the sound of popping steam, and a "rumble like the gathering force of a cyclone" as the trains gathered speed. Faster and faster they went, down the inclines toward each other, with whistles blowing and explosives that had been set in the track thundering in their wake. In barely 2 minutes, the trains reached an estimated 45 mph.

Seconds before impact, some frightened spectators looked away, but everyone in attendance felt the ground shake when the engines met.

First came a deafening explosion. Then, almost instantly, clouds of smoke, dust, and scalding steam from the engines' burst boilers filled the air. Wood splinters and steel fragments as tiny as postage stamps and as large as wheels rained down on the terrified and screaming crowd. The cap of a smokestack flew across the valley and embedded itself in the ground. A 2-inch bolt landed in the eye of a photographer. Two pieces of heavy steel brake chain soared through the air like flying serpents. One cracked the skull of a 19-year-old boy,

killing him. At least one other person also died. Many people suffered injuries. The crews survived by jumping from the trains at the beginning of the run.

The locomotives were demolished. Of the boxcars, only the last one on each train escaped without damage.

◀ After the explosion, a crowd gathered to view the wreck. In all, only five cars remained upright, and two remained undamaged.

Railroad officials had expected the locomotives to push each other up, on end, upon impact. Instead, they telescoped horizontally, flattening each other. William Crush was fired, but he was rehired the next day. The railroad cleaned up the mess and, by nightfall, only a few hints of what had happened remained, including the name of the place. It was called Crush only for that day.

Train collisions as entertainment continued, at fairs, until the 1920s. A roadside marker was placed near the site of the Crash at Crush in 1977.

MUSICAL MAYHEM
Ragtime composer Scott Joplin composed a march called "The Great Crush Collision." To listen to it, go to Almanac4kids.com/crush.

Animal Families

ANIMAL	MALE	FEMALE	YOUNG
Ant	Male-ant (reproductive)	Queen (reproductive), worker (nonreproductive)	Antling
Antelope	Ram	Ewe	Calf, fawn, kid, yearling
Bear	Boar, he-bear	Sow, she-bear	Cub
Beaver	Boar	Sow	Kit, kitten
Bee	Drone	Queen or queen bee (reproductive), worker (nonreproductive)	Larva
Buffalo	Bull	Cow	Calf, yearling, spike-bull (m)
Camel	Bull	Cow	Calf, colt
Caribou	Bull, stag, hart	Cow, doe	Calf, fawn
Cat	Tom, tomcat, gib, gibcat, boarcat, ramcat	Tabby, grimalkin, malkin, pussy, queen	Kitten, kit, kitling, kitty, pussy
Cattle	Bull	Cow	Calf, stot, yearling, bullcalf (m), heifer (f)
Chicken	Rooster, cock, stag, chanticleer	Hen, partlet, biddy	Chick, chicken, poult, cockerel (m), pullet (f)
Deer	Buck, stag	Doe	Fawn
Dog	Dog	Bitch	Whelp, puppy
Donkey	Jack, jackass	Jenny	Foal
Duck	Drake, stag	Duck	Duckling, flapper
Elephant	Bull	Cow	Calf
Fox	Dog	Vixen	Kit, pup, cub

(m) = male   (f) = female

COLLECTIVE

Colony, nest, army, state, swarm

Herd

Sleuth, sloth

Family, colony

Swarm, grist, cluster, nest, hive, erst

Troop, herd, gang

Flock, train, caravan

Herd

Clowder, clutter (kindle or kendle of kittens)

Drove, herd

Flock, run, brood, clutch, peep

Herd, leash

Pack (cry or mute of hounds, leash of greyhounds)

Pace, drove, herd

Brace, team, paddling, raft, bed, flock, flight

Herd

Leash, skulk, cloud, troop

CONTINUED

Animal Families (continued)

ANIMAL	MALE	FEMALE	YOUNG
Giraffe	Bull	Cow	Calf
Goat	Buck, billy, billie, billie-goat, he-goat	She-goat, nanny, nannie, nannie-goat	Kid
Goose	Gander, stag	Goose, dame	Gosling
Horse	Stallion, stag, horse, stud	Mare, dam	Colt, foal, stot, stag (m), filly (f), hog-colt (m),
Kangaroo	Buck	Doe	Joey
Leopard	Leopard	Leopardess	Cub
Lion	Lion, tom	Lioness, she-lion	Shelp, cub, lionet
Moose	Bull	Cow	Calf
Partridge	Cock	Hen	Cheeper
Pig	Boar	Sow	Shoat, pig, piglet, suckling
Quail	Cock	Hen	Cheeper, chick, squealer
Reindeer	Buck	Doe	Fawn
Seal	Bull	Cow	Whelp, pup, cub, bachelor (m)
Sheep	Buck, ram, male-sheep, mutton	Ewe, dam	Lamb, lambkin, shearling, yearling, cosset, hog
Swan	Cob	Pen	Cygnet
Termite	King	Queen	Nymph
Walrus	Bull	Cow	Cub
Whale	Bull	Cow	Calf
Zebra	Stallion	Mare	Colt (m), filly (f), foal

(m) = male   (f) = female

COLLECTIVE

Herd, corps, troop

Tribe, trip, flock, herd

Flock (on land), skein (in flight), gaggle or
   plump (on water)

Haras, stable, remuda, stud, herd, string, field,
   set, pair, team

Mob, troop, herd

Leap

Pride, troop, flock, sawt, souse

Herd

Covey

Drift, sounder, herd, trip (litter of pigs),
   farrow (litter of pigs)

Bevy, covey

Herd

Pod, herd, trip, rookery, harem

Flock, drove, hirsel, trip, pack

Herd, team, bank, wege, bevy

Colony, nest, swarm, brood

Pod, herd

Gam, pod, school, herd

Herd

How old Is Your Dog?

Multiplying your dog's age by seven is easy, but it isn't very accurate. This more carefully graded system piles the equivalent human years onto a dog's life more quickly during the dog's rapid growth to maturity. One "dog year" equals 4 "human years" from ages 2–14 and 2½ "human years" thereafter.

DOG AGE	EQUIVALENT HUMAN AGE
6 months	10 years
1 year	15
2 years	24
3	28
4	32
5	36
6	40
7	44
8	48
9	52
10	56
11	60
12	64
13	68
14	72
15	74½
16	77
17	79½
18	82
19	84½
20	87
21	89½
22	92
23	94½
24	97
25	99½
26	102
27	104½
28	107
29	109½
30	112

WHAT ARE YOU AFRAID OF?

pho·bi·a   **'fō-bē-ə**   *noun*

1. A phobia is a persistent, abnormal, or irrational fear of a specific thing or situation that compels one to avoid the feared stimulus.
2. A phobia is also strong fear, dislike, or aversion.

PHOBIA SUBJECT	PHOBIA TERM
Animals	Zoophobia
Beards	Pogonophobia
Birds	Ornithophobia
Blood	Hematophobia
Choking	Pnigophobia
Crossing bridges	Gephyrophobia
Crowds	Ochlophobia
Dreams	Oneirophobia
Flowers	Anthophobia
Flying	Aerophobia
Garlic	Alliumphobia
Germs	Mysophobia
Haircuts	Tonsurphobia
Height	Acrophobia
Height, being near something of great	Batophobia
Hospitals	Nosocomephobia
Illness	Nosemaphobia
Lakes	Limnophobia
Lightning and thunder	Astraphobia
Long words	Sesquipedalopphobia
Men	Androphobia
Money	Chrometophobia

PHOBIA SUBJECT	PHOBIA TERM
Night, darkness	Nyctophobia
Open or public places	Agoraphobia
Shadows	Sciophobia
Snakes	Ophidiophobia
Sun	Heliophobia
Touch	Haptophobia
Train travel	Siderodromophobia
Water	Hydrophobia
Women	Gynophobia

U.S. Presidential Succession

If the President of the United States were to die, quit, or become disabled, the Vice President would be sworn in as President. If the Vice President were unable to perform, the Speaker of the House would take the office, and so on. Here is the order ➡

1. Vice President
2. Speaker of the House
3. President Pro Tempore of the Senate
4. Secretary of State
5. Secretary of the Treasury
6. Secretary of Defense
7. Attorney General
8. Secretary of the Interior
9. Secretary of Agriculture
10. Secretary of Commerce
11. Secretary of Labor
12. Secretary of Health and Human Services
13. Secretary of Housing and Urban Development
14. Secretary of Transportation
15. Secretary of Energy
16. Secretary of Education
17. Secretary of Veterans Affairs
18. Secretary of Homeland Security

To assume the presidency, a person must also meet the legal requirements to serve as President:

- **be a natural-born citizen of the United States**
- **be 35 or older**
- **have been a resident of the United States for at least 14 years**

METRIC MATH

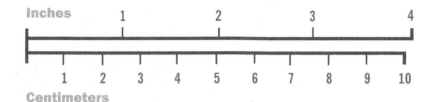

Metric Conversion

ENGLISH MEASURE	X THIS NUMBER	= METRIC EQUIVALENT	METRIC MEASURE	x THIS NUMBER	= ENGLISH EQUIVALENT
inch	2.54	centimeter		0.39	inch
foot	30.48	centimeter		0.033	foot
yard	0.91	meter		1.09	yard
mile	1.61	kilometer		0.62	mile
square inch	6.45	square centimeter		0.15	square inch
square foot	0.09	square meter		10.76	square foot
square yard	0.8	square meter		1.2	square yard
square mile	0.84	square kilometer		0.39	square mile
acre	0.4	hectare		2.47	acre
ounce	28.0	gram		0.035	ounce
pound	0.45	kilogram		2.2	pound
short ton (2,000 pounds)	0.91	metric ton		1.10	short ton
ounce	30.0	milliliter		0.034	ounce
pint	0.47	liter		2.1	pint
quart	0.95	liter		1.06	quart
gallon	3.8	liter		0.26	gallon

If you know the English measurement and want to convert it to metric, multiply it by the number in the orange column (*example:* 1 inch equals 2.54 centimeters). If you know the metric measurement, multiply it by the number in the green column (*example:* 2 meters equals 2.18 yards).

Rules of Introduction

Manners

Countless situations call for introductions. To carry out a "proper" introduction easily, just remember to say first the name of the person who is having someone introduced to them. For example, say: "Mary, this is Tom Smith. Tom, Mary Jones." Here are some basic guidelines to help you know who to introduce to whom.

A man ➡ to a woman

A young person ➡ to an older person

A student in your own school ➡ to a student in another school

A nonofficial person ➡ to an official person

A new teacher ➡ to an "old" teacher

A fellow student ➡ to a visiting student

Even if you can't remember the proper order of introduction, forget names, or make another mistake in your introduction, it is a far greater blunder to neglect this social courtesy altogether.

Matter

Having Tea With the Queen?

On the off chance that you may have the honor of conversing with members of the British royal family or members of the nobility, or you are role-playing, use these forms of address:

To the queen or king ➡ Your Majesty

To the monarch's spouse, children, and siblings ➡ Your Royal Highness

To nephews, nieces, and cousins of the monarch ➡ Your Highness

To a duke or duchess, if you are also among the nobility ➡ Duke or Duchess

To a duke or duchess, if you are a commoner ➡ Your Grace

To a bishop of the Church of England ➡ My Lord

To an earl, marquis, or viscount ➡ Lord
(An earl and a marquis are usually "of" someplace, but you don't say the "of"; just say "Lord Derby" for the Earl of Derby.)

To a marchioness, countess, viscountess, or baroness ➡ Lady
(As for "Lord," you don't say the "of.")

To a baronet or knight ➡ Sir
(Also use his first name, as in "Sir Thomas Lipton.")

To the wife of a baronet or knight ➡ Lady

Birthstones

JANUARY: garnet	JULY: ruby
FEBRUARY: amethyst	AUGUST: peridot
MARCH: aquamarine	SEPTEMBER: sapphire
APRIL: diamond	OCTOBER: opal
MAY: emerald	NOVEMBER: yellow topaz
JUNE: pearl	DECEMBER: turquoise

ACKNOWLEDGMENTS

PICTURE CREDITS

ABBREVIATIONS:
GCNY—The Granger Collection, New York
GI—Getty Images
JI—Jupiter Images
NASA—National Aeronautics and Space
Administration
NASA/JPL—National Aeronautics and Space
Administration/Jet Propulsion Laboratory
NOAA—National Oceanic and Atmospheric
Administration
SS—SuperStock, Inc.

The editors acknowledge Jupiter Images Unlimited as the source for numerous images that appear in this publication.

Front cover: (Vegetable face) Garry Gay/GI. (Boy with frog) Burke/Triolo Productions/JI. (Girl with watering can) Ariel Skelley/JI.

Introduction: 8: (Center) Stephen O. Muskie.

Calendar: 10-11: (All) GCNY. 16-17: (Top) Fortuni/JI. 16: (Center) Daisy Martinez. 17: (Bottom left) Ulterior Epicure. 20: (Top) Dale Hurren. (Center) Brand X/SS. (Bottom) GCNY.

Astronomy: 23: NASA and The Hubble Heritage Team. 24-25: (Bottom) NASA/Jeff Hester and Paul Scowen [Arizona State University]. 25: (Top) NASA, ESA, and R. Humphreys [University of Minnesota]. 26-27: (Top) David A. Hardy/www.astroart.org/STFC. 26: (Left) NASA and Jon Morse [University of Colorado]. (Bottom right) NASA, ESA, P. Challis, and R. Kirshner [Harvard-Smithsonian Center for Astrophysics]. 27: (Bottom) NASA/Jeffrey Kenney and Elizabeth Yale [Yale University]. 28: Art Montes De Oca/GI. 30: (Diagrams) Margo Letourneau. 32: Steele Hill/NASA. 35: (Top) Dr. Robert Mallozzi/University of Alabama, Huntsville, and Marshall Flight Center. 37: (Bottom) NASA. 38: (Top) NASA/JPL. 39: (Top and center) NASA. (Bottom) NASA/JPL. 40: (All) NASA/JPL. 41: (All) NASA.

Weather: 42-43: Mike Hollingshead. 44: (Diagram) Margo Letourneau. (Center right) NOAA/courtesy Jackson County Historical Society, Murphysboro, Illinois. 45: (Left) NOAA. 46: (Top) Michael Ochs Archives/Corbis. (Center right and bottom right) NOAA. 47: NOAA. 48:

(Top) Nikki Mans from http://whimsylove.etsy.com. 50: (Illustration) Abby Carter. 54: Wilson Bentley Digital Archives/Jericho Historical Society/www.snowflakebentley.com. 55: Image Source/GI. 58: http://snowcrystals.com. 59: Rachel Kipka.

Nature: 60-61: NaGen Imaging/JI. 62: (Top left) NaGen Imaging/JI. (Top right and center right) Natural History Museum, Institute of Jamaica. 64-65: (Bottom) Brian J. Skerry/National Geographic Image Collection. 66-68: (Illustrations) Kim Kurki. 69: Maria Corcacas.

The Environment: 74: (Bottom) Office of Fossil Energy, U.S. Department of Energy. 76: (All) Foster & Partners. 77: (Top) www.nycgarbage.com. (Center) Marisa Lo Certo. (Bottom) www.borisbally.com. 79: (Center left) Warren Gretz/DOE/NREL. 80: Kawakahi Kaeo Amina. 81: (Bottom) http://zeropollutionmotors.us.

In the Garden: 82: (Top) Cindy Atwater. 83: (Right) Louise Reid. (Left) Chad Fust. 84: (Top) David Goldfarb. (Bottom) Ingo Arndt/Minden Pictures/National Geographic Image Collection. 85: Jef Poskanzer. 86: (Top left and top right) Territorial Seed Company. 87: (Top left) Territorial Seed Company. 88: (Illustration) Renée Quintal Daily. 89: (Center) Karen Fenton/Stock.xchng. 90: (Center) Holly Lowe. (Bottom left) Laura Carmelita Bellmont. 92: (Bottom) JI. 95: Garry Gay/GI. 96: Ted Dreger. 97: (Center) Laura Vlahovich. (Bottom) Rosie Green. 98: (Center) Stockbyte/SS. (Bottom) ImageState-Pictor/JI. 99: (Top) Lisa Romerein/JI. (Bottom) Royalty-Free/Corbis/JI. 100-101: (Illustrations) Eldon Doty.

On the Farm: 102-103: Mauritius/SS. 102: (Bottom) Zia Soleil/GI. 103: (Bottom) National Geographic/SS. 105: Tim Flach/GI. 108: Zachary Huang. 112: (Center) Scott Bauer/USDA Agricultural Research Service. (Bottom) Reuters. 113: (Top) Eileen M. Flanagan. 114: Iowa State University. 115: (Top) Michelle C. Dunn. (Center) Allison Newhouse.

Sports: 122: Maine State Museum (hand tinting by Margo Letourneau). 123: (Top) Phillips Historical Society. 124: (Bottom) Maine State Museum (hand tinting by Margo Letourneau). 127: (Center) Boston Public Library. (Bottom left) http://runningpast.com. 128: Library and Archives of Canada.

129: Library and Archives of Canada. 130: Radius Images/JI. 131: Bananastock/JI.

Pets: 132: Corbis/JI. 133: (Center) Oxford Scientific/JI. 134: (Center bottom) Mike Long. 136: (Bottom) RubberBall/SS. 138: Cheryl Ward. 139: Dave Costlow, Rocky Mountain Adventures. 140: (Top) Monica Macdonald. (Bottom) Shelley Morrison.

Food: 142: (Top) Sybil Sassoon/Robert Harding/JI. (Bottom) Dinodia Photo Library/JI. 144: (Top) North Wind Picture Archives. 147: Tim Hawley/JI. 148: (Center) blueduck/JI. (Bottom) Gary Moss/JI. 149: (Top) Jose Luis Pelaez Inc./JI.

Health: 153: Nucleus Medical Art, Inc./GI. 156: (Top right) GCNY. (Center left) GCNY. (Bottom left) GCNY. (Bottom right) Bettmann/Corbis. 159: GCNY (detail from a painting by Dean Cornwell). 160: (Center) Chad Baker/GI.

Amusement: 162–163: (Illustration) Eldon Doty. 164: Kent M. Farnsworth/http://philotfarnsworth.com. 165: (Center) Kent M. Farnsworth. (Bottom) Bettmann/Corbis. 166: Kent M. Farnsworth. 168: Tatyana Jula. 170–171: (Illustration) RobRoy Menzies. 172: (Right) Erik and Martin Dahinden. (Illustration, bottom) Steven Russell Black. 174–175: (All) GCNY. 176: Texas Collection, Baylor University. 177: (Center) GCNY.

CONTRIBUTORS

Jeff Baker: The Kid Who Invented TV, 164. **Jack Burnett:** Backyard Olympics, 130. **Alice Cary:** Catch the Wind, 48; The Chilling Tale of the Snowflake Man, 54; Let It Snow!, 59; Trash Talk, 70; Ways to Go!, 78; All About the All-American Bird, 102; Butter Fingers!, 113; Baseball's "Cyclone," 120; Hooked on the Outdoors, 122; Born to Run, 126; Spilling the Beans About Chocolate, 142; Honey, Eat Your Ants!, 150; Say What?, 152; Bigfoot or Big Fake?, 170. **Mare-Anne Jarvela:** Something Is Eating the Moon and Sun!, 28; Giant Jupiter and Its Many Moons, 38; Twisters!, 42; Grow Plants Under Glass, 90; Name That Vegetable, 95; Hairs to You!, 160. **Martie Majoros:** Many Moons, 10; The Powers of Attraction, 32; Cloudy, With a Chance of Fish, 50; Jaws!, 60; Pet-iculars, 136. **Sandy Newton:**
Pets at Work, 138. **Sarah Perreault:** Dining by the Calendar, 16; When Mules Rule (and Other Noteworthy Holidays), 20; You Are My Sunshine, 86; The Beet Goes On, 92; Rabbit Roundup, 132; A Slice of History, 146. **Staton Rabin:** Scare Tactics, 100. **Janice Stillman:** Where Did This Almanac Come From?, 8; Itching to Know About Fleas?, 137; Quick Fixes, 157; The Man With the See-Through Stomach, 158; Slowpoke's Last-Place Win, 162; How to Get Rich Without Doing Any Work, 167; The Toughest Cowboy Ever, 168; The Crash at Crush, 174. **Heidi Stonehill:** The Origin of Day Names, 13; What It Takes to Be a Star, 22; Far Out!, 36; Beating the Heat, 66; Hold Your Nose!, 82; Scrubbable, Lovable Loofah, 96; The Buzz on Bees, 108; Got Gear?, 116.

Content not cited here is adapted from *The Old Farmer's Almanac* archives or appears in the public domain. Every effort has been made to correctly attribute all material. If any errors have been unwittingly committed, they will be corrected in a future edition.

INDEX

A
activities
  bake beets, 94
  celebrate holidays, 21
  collect iron in cereal, 35
  compete in backyard "Olympics," 130–131
  grow beets, 93
  grow loofah (luffa) 96–98
  grow plants under glass, 90–91
  grow a sunflower tower, 88–89
  magnetize an object, 35
  make loofah snowflakes, 98–99
  make paper snowflakes, 59
  make a wind chime, 48–49
  match months with Moon names, 12
  match tales with tails, 135
  name the vegetable, 95
address, forms of, 187
almanac, 8–9
Amundsen, Roald, 145
Amusement, 162–177
animal names, 178–181
Astronomy, 22–41
  eclipse(s), 28–31
  International Space Station, 37
  Jupiter, 38–41
  magnetic field(s), 32–33
  planet rotation, 36
  star(s), 22–27, 36

B
baseball
  catcher's mitt, 117–118
  Cy Young (plus Award), 120–121
  fastball, world record, 118
  perfect game, 121
Beaumont, Dr. William, 158–159
Beethoven, Ludwig van, 156
beet(s), 92–94
  baking, 94
  dehydrated, 94
  dye in foods, 94
  growing, 93
  in space, 94
  pickled, 94
Bentley, Wilson, 54–57
Bigfoot, 170–173
bird(s), 69, 89, 102–107, 139
bird feed, 69
  sunflower seeds, 89
birthstone(s), 187
black hole(s), 27
butter, 113–115
  cow lady, 114
  "fingers," 115
  princess(es), 115
  sculpting, 113–115

C
Calendar, 10–21
  almanac is a, 8
  dining by, 16–19
  full Moon names, 10–11, 12
catcher's mitt, 117–118
chocolate, 142–145
  and pets, 145
  beans, 142
  in history, 144–145
  in products, 145
  making, 143
  science, 144
Columbus, Christopher
  and chocolate, 144
  and total eclipse, 31
  and turkeys, 106
collective names, animal, 178–181
corpse flower, 85
Cortés, Hernando, 144
cowboy, the toughest ever, 168–169
crash, at Crush, 174–177
Crosby, Cornelia Thurza, 122–125
Crush, William George, 174–177
Cy Young Award, 121

D
day(s)
  celebrated with food, 16–19
  Cinco de Mayo, 20
  Juneteenth, 20
  "fun," 20–21
  length on Jupiter, 36
  length on Venus, 36
  Mule, 20
  names, origin of, 13
  why the week has seven, 14–15
Death Valley, 68
decomposition rate(s), trash, 75
desert animals, 66–68

E
ear(s), 152–156
  anatomy, 152, 153
  care, 154–155
  deafness, 156
  smallest bone, 153
  wax, 152
eclipse(s), 28–31
"eco city," Dongtan, China, 76
Edison, Thomas, 156
energy sources
  air, 80
  algae, 79
  biofuels, 78–79
  chicken fat, 80
  gasoline, 78
  grassoline, 79
  ethanol (corn), 79
  oil, diesel, 78

peanut, 78
poop, 81
waste vegetable oil (WVO), 80
Environment, The, 70–81

F
falcon(s), 141
Farm, On the, 102–115
Farnsworth, Philo T., 164–168
fear(s), 183
fish
  pilot fish, 65
  raining, 51, 52, 53
  remoras, 64–65
  sharks, 60–65
fishing, 122–125
flea(s), 137
Food, 142–151
  beets, 92–94
  chocolate, 142–145
  dining by the calendar, 16–19
  insects, edible, 150–151
  loofah, 99
  pizza, 146–149
  sunflower seeds, 89
football helmet, 116–117
Franklin, Benjamin, 107
frog(s), raining, 51, 52, 53

G
Galilei, Galileo, 38
Garden, In the, 82–101
geese, 141

H
hair(s), 160–161
  care, 160
  color, 161
hare(s), 134
Health, 152–161
Hillary, Sir Edmund, 145, 173
honeybee(s)
  "bee's knees," 112
  facts, 112

honey, 111, 112
  keeping, 110-111, 112
  mite(s), 112
  predators, 112
  sting(s), 108
horse(s), 138
  gait guide, 163
  miniature, 141
  Slowpoke, 162–163
Hoy, William Ellsworth "Dummy," 156

I
insects, edible, 150–151
International Space Station, 37
introductions, rules of 186

J
Jupiter, 38–41

K
Keller, Helen, 156

L
llama(s), 140–141
Longboat, Tom, 126–129
loofah (luffa), 96–99
Low, Juliette, 156

M
magnet(s), 32–35
  discovery of, 34
  in animals, 34
  magnetar, 35
  magnetic
    field, 32–33
    poles, 33
    storms, 32
manners, 186–187
marathon, Boston, 127, 128–129
Matlin, Marlee, 156
metric conversion, 185
month(s), 10–11, 12
  birthstone(s), 187

dining by, 16–19
holidays, 16–19, 20, 21
and Native American full Moon names, 10–11, 12
moon(s)
  in eclipse, 28–31
  Jupiter's, 38–41
  names, Native American full, 10–11, 12
  rabbit, in the, 134
morning glory, 89
mummy, 169

N
Nature, 60–69
Norgay, Tenzing, 145

P
peat pot, 96
Pet(s), 132–141
  and chocolate, 145
  and fleas, 137
  at work, 138–141
  cat(s), 136, 137, 140–141, 145
  dog(s), 136, 137, 141, 145, 182
  horse, 138
  llama(s), 140–141
  pigeon(s), homing, 139
  rabbit(s), 132–135
phobia(s), 183
pilot fish, 65
pizza, 146–149
  in history, 146–148
  personalities, 148
  toppings, 149
  world records, 147
planet(s)
  rotation, 36
  from the Greek word, 36
  Jupiter, 38–41
plasma gasification, 74
presidential succession, U.S., 184

R
rabbit(s)
lore, 134–135
raining oddities, 51–53
recycled
cans, 70–71
cars, 72
electronics, 74
glass, 72
plastic, 73
trash for cash, 77
remedies, 157
remora(s), 64–65

S
Sasquatch, 170, 171
scarecrow(s), 100–101
Scott, Robert Falcon, 145
shark(s), 60–65
items found in, 60, 62, 63
uses of body parts, 65
skunk cabbage, 82–84
snowflake(s), 54–58
guide to, 58
"Snowflake Man," 54–57
soccer ball, 118–119
first game with, 119
Sonoran Desert, 68
Sports, 116–131
baseball, 117–118, 120–121
fishing, 122–125
football, 116–117
gear, 116–119
"Olympics," 130–131
running, 126–129
soccer, 118–119
star(s), 22–27
birth of, 24
brightness, 22
color, 23–26
fading, 26
magnetar, 35

size, 25–27
twinkle, 36
stinking corpse lily, 85
stomach, man with the
see-through, 158–159
Sun
in eclipse, 28–31
spin, 36
sunflower(s), 86–89
growing 88–89
seed, 87, 89
world record, 87

T
terrarium, 90–91
invention of, 91
plants for, 91
Thomas, Robert B., 8–9
thunderstorm, 44, 52
tornado(es), 42–47, 52
train accident(s), 174–177
trash
decomposition rate(s), 75
plasma gasification, 74
to cash, 77
turkey(s), 102–107
and Benjamin
Franklin, 107
body parts, 105
bowling score, 107
eating, 104
presidential pardon of, 104
raising, 102, 104, 105, 106
"talk," 106
trot (dance), 107
TV dinner, 107
turkey vulture, 67, 107
TV, the kid who invented, 164–166

U
Useful Things, 178–187

V
vegetable(s)
beet, 92–94
loofah (luffa), 96–99

W
Wakefield, Ruth, 145
Weather, 42–59
heat, how desert
animals cope with, 66–68
the hottest place in
North America, 68
weather proverbs
bees, 110–111
green sky, 47
hair, 161
fish, 53
frogs, 53
snowflake(s), 55, 56
wind, 49
week has seven days,
why the, 14–15
weekday names, origin
of, 13
wind, 45–49, 52
windiest places
in Canada, 49
in the United States, 49
work
pets at, 138–141
how to get rich without
doing any, 167

Y
Young, Denton True
"Cy," 120–121

Z
zero-carbon city, Masdar
City, United Arab
Emirates, 76